AF552672

Body & Soul

EMOTIONS AND STATES OF BEING IN PHOTOGRAPHS AND VERSE

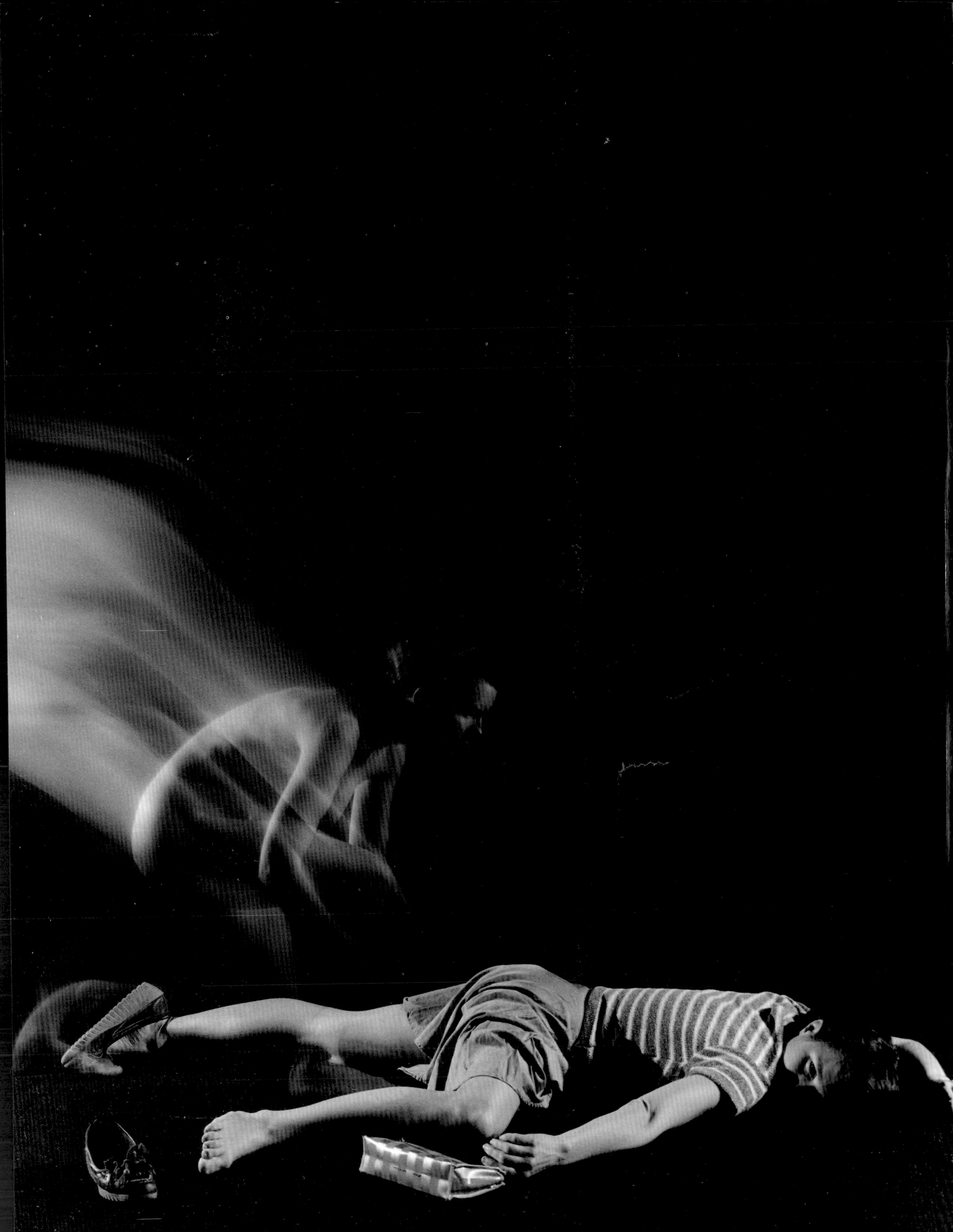

Body & Soul

EMOTIONS AND STATES OF BEING IN PHOTOGRAPHS AND VERSE

JAMES ANDREW MITCHELL

WITH SELECTED QUOTATIONS

PLEASANT VIEW PRESS

To John & Kay with thanks for your generosity

Enjoy!

Published in the United States of America
by Pleasant View Press, Camden, Maine
Printed by Camden Printing, Camden, Maine

This book was designed by Alexandra Caponigro
and has been set in Adobe Garamond type.

Cover Picture
ANGUISH
performed by Eleni Koenka
Black and white silver print, 11 by 14 inches.

Frontispiece
BODY AND SOUL
performed by Eleni Koenka
Black and white silver print, 11 by 14 inches.

Library of Congress Cataloging-in-Publication Data
Mitchell, James Andrew
Body & Soul
Emotions and States of Being
in photographs and verse
with selected quotations
Includes index of authors
Supt. of Docs. no.: 99-93122
isbn 0-9670878-0-5

FIRST EDITION

PLEASANT VIEW PRESS

Post Office Box 778, Barnestown Road, Camden, Maine 04843
Fax: 207 - 236 - 0677
E-Mail: pvpress@mint.net

Contents

List of Plates

WITH QUOTATIONS

List of Authors and Subjects

For our daughters,

Beth and Nora

Who are both teachers,

One of life's highest callings.

Preface

JAMES ANDREW MITCHELL

While this body of work depicts emotions and states of being, it is really about art and various forms of artistic expression. It is about bringing together a number of art forms to present images which impact our feelings — images with an emotional story. Dance, mime, acting, poetry, and photography, or more properly in this situation, painting with light on photographic film, are all involved.

Dance is one of our oldest, most beautiful, and highest forms of the performing arts. As Havelock Ellis wrote, "It is no mere translation or abstraction from life; it is life itself." So too is acting a powerful and often emotional art which sometimes can appear to be more real than life. Mime is an ancient Greek and Roman art form which in more modern guise has been altered to portray emotions and situations through various actions and gestures without the use of language. Separately or combined, these arts are employed here through the use of photographic images to depict emotions and states of being.

These pictures, while they are meant to stand alone, are reinforced in this work by verse and quotations from poets and philosophers throughout history. If a picture is said to be worth many words, the art of poetry is the very distillation of words. William Wordsworth once wrote;

> *I have said that poetry is the spontaneous overflow of powerful feelings; it takes its origin from emotions recollected in tranquility.*

Many of the images in this book expand the envelope of normal still photography. In mime acting several visual images are often used to adequately describe and portray the development of an emotion. So too in dance. Thus I have used open shutter and multiple images on the same negative, sometimes in combination, to present these. Strong emotions also call for strong, sometimes extreme lighting. Many of these pictures use light as paint to both reflect the emotional content as well as to reduce unnecessary detail.

Because this is now the age of digital imaging where pictures may be easily manipulated, I believe that it is useful to restate a fact, which may become obvious as you read the text, that none of the images in this book have been manipulated, nor has there been any layering of negatives. Each image has been produced on a single negative much in the same way that a painter works — one figure at a time in the case of multiple figures, or with streaks of light as they have been reflected from the figure where an open shutter has been combined with movement. The only place where digital imaging has been utilized for this book is in the scanning of the photographs to prepare film and plates for the printing process.

The use of costume or clothing has been deliberately minimized in this body of work for two reasons. First, I believe that emotions and states of being are essentially timeless; clothing can only get in the way of that quality unless there is some specific need, or where its use will enhance the image. Second, the human form, particularly the female form, is beautiful in itself and so does not usually require adornment to contribute to the impact of the image except for the normal requirements of modesty. The ancients knew this and used it effectively, and for that reason I have utilized a version of the toga in some of these pictures.

I know that the interpretation of emotions can be a very personal experience from which different viewers receive different messages as to what the image says to them, and that these in turn may differ from my interpretation. The images, quotations, and descriptions in this work represent my personal view. Some are quite clear in their message; a few are certainly ambiguous. If you receive a different message from the body language or expression, I welcome your view as I hope you will accept mine. For this reason there is an effort to de-emphasize titles.

Finally, I wish to share my thoughts on the organization of the work for your viewing and reading, some comments on what has or has not been included, and a very brief discussion on the selection of quotations.

The plates and verse in this book might have been organized in a number of ways — chronologically, by artist, by type of subject, or even by type of photograph. None of these were used. Instead, I have chosen to present these in a progression of emotional content; that is, beginning with neutral to calm feelings, moving then to increasingly strong positive emotions, moving next to strongly negative emotional content, and finally returning to more neutral feelings. It is as if we started our day content, got ready to meet the outside world, met the person of our dreams, became deliriously involved, were rejected, went through the emotional turmoil of anger, hate, and despair, lost someone dear to us, and then finally, tired and resigned, were rewarded with a moment of tenderness.

This book represents only a sample of the feeling words in our vocabulary. My hope, however, has been to hit a number of the high points around which many fairly similar emotions are clustered. Beyond this, I have chosen to present a small selection of images which are closer to states of being than to emotions, three of which are at the end of the book, all based on the beauty and power of dance.

In original drafts of this book some explanations of various images were included with the quotations. Several reviewers, including Hank Ward who wrote the *Afterword*, told me they found this detracted from the power of the images and quotations standing alone. For this reason, I have moved these to a section at the end titled *Author's Comments*. Some viewing this work may have a specific interest in photography, so I have also added a short discourse *On Making These Images.*

Questions have been raised as to whether the images or quotations in this work came first. The answer is both. For a number of the images, I have first picked a word, found some pertinent verse, then worked to execute a photograph to fit. For some others, I had the word and idea for a picture, completed it, then found a verse or quotation. And for a very few, the picture and verse both came from my imagination.

This has been a labor of love, not only to explore the combining of various art forms, but also to enhance our appreciation of the power of artistic expression combining visual arts with the written word. I hope you, the viewer, will share some of this feeling.

Camden, Maine
December, 1998

Acknowledgments

This work would not have been possible without the enthusiastic participation and collaboration of four talented and artistic individuals. This book is as much theirs as mine because it is their art that has made these images possible. Each deserve special recognition:

Eleni Koenka of Penobscot, Maine, both for the number of pictures in which she has participated, and for her excited and eager support. She not only provided her very real talents in dance and acting, but also helped to improve on the results through repeated retakes;

Marguerite Mathews of Portsmouth, New Hampshire, who first demonstrated to me the power of mime in the interpretation of emotions, and who gave generously of her time and acting abilities in the early portion of this project, as well as lending me the use of the Pontine Movement Theatre of which she is the co-artistic director;

Anne Sauvé of Kittery Point, Maine, who contributed some extraordinary acting ability as a mime actress which further developed the work during this early period;

and *Susan Corinne Abbott* of Montville, Maine, who joined me at the invitation of Eleni Koenka, unstintingly contributing her very real artistic abilities which helped complete the work for this book.

Beyond these four, a number of people have provided encouragement, advice, and constructive criticism along the way which has been of tremendous help. While I can't mention them all, my heartfelt thanks to:

Betsy Broun, Director of the National Museum of American Art, Smithsonian Institution, for her early encouragement to proceed, particularly along more experimental directions;

Bruce Brown, a teacher and Curator of Maine Coast Artists, Rockport, Maine, who felt the work worthy of inclusion in several juried shows, and has graciously contributed the *Foreword*;

Henry Ward, MD, who retired to Maine after many years of the practice of psychoanalysis, reviewed and commented on the work, and has graciously contributed the *Afterword*;

Mildred Schmertz, an architect and journalist, former editor-in-chief of *Architectural Record,* for her penetrating comments on editorial direction;

and *Lolly Mitchell,* my wife and best friend, who has not only been continuously involved in supporting this project, but also provided wise counsel as well as editing.

Quotations is this book come from a number of sources, the primary ones being the Home Book of Verse *and* Home Book of Quotations, *editions of 1952 and* Bartlett's Familiar Quotations, *edition of 1992. Additional inspiration has been drawn from works by Homer, Shakespeare, Kipling, Wordsworth and* Modern Japanese Literature.

Foreword

BRUCE BROWN

Throughout his life, Jim Mitchell has loved the camera. He picked up his first one as a boy at home outside of Philadelphia. Self-taught, he "learned by doing" on his favorite Kodak Recomar, a pre-World War II instrument complete with bellows. He continued to make black and white images throughout his school years and as a pilot trainee in the Army Air Corps. A busy twenty-five year career, first as a design engineer for Union Carbide Corporation and later as senior international consultant in industrial development, energy, and alternative fuels for Arthur D. Little, Inc. allowed just enough time for shooting "ordinary travel photographs" as he describes them on extended assignments in the Middle East and Korea. Likewise as the founder and general partner of Sakonnet Vineyards, Rhode Island's first licensed winery and vineyard, from 1975 to 1987, Jim found little time for pursuing his favorite hobby.

A year later, Jim and his wife, Lolly, decided to retire to Maine. At their best, retirement years offer opportunities to turn at last to previous enthusiasms that deepen one's understanding and appreciation for what is good in life. Two significant spiritual journeys emerged. One led along the northern Atlantic coast. Every summer Jim and Lolly respond to the inevitable pull of the sea beckoning them from their enviable perch at Pleasant View Farm overlooking Camden several miles distant. They set off on *Kintore*, a handsome 37 foot motorsailer which Jim helped design and build on an open-ended odyssey putting into harbor wherever nature's or their own whims dictate. Theirs is the world where earth and water meet in spectacular fashion to explore at a leisurely pace.

The second journey has been more introspective and limited to the confines of the photographic studio and darkroom. Once in Maine, the time had come to pursue photography seriously. It was time for the exacting scientist to open himself up to the aesthetic side of himself. Jim signed on for courses at the renowned Maine Photographic Workshops in 1989, 1991, and 1993. In 1991 Jim embarked on a project lasting seven years. The result is *Body & Soul*, a photographic essay combining Jim's long abiding appreciation for the written word, the dramatic arts, dance and mime, feminine beauty, and most notably, the artistic possibilities of photography itself.

Each photograph herein defines a specific emotion or state of being taken largely from the canons of memorable literature. While the marrying of photographic image to the printed word seems a worthy enterprise in itself, an even more potent marriage of intent and aesthetic import is implicit in this endeavor — the relationship between the photographer and the "subjects" photographed. *Body & Soul* is a collaboration among Jim and four partners at various times: dancer/actresses Eleni Koenka and Susan Abbott, and the mime actresses Marguerite Mathews and Anne Sauvé. This successful collaboration depended not only on the very considerable interpretive abilities of the four women, but equally on Jim's own instinctive ability to capture the exact psychological moment with his shutter. It was a question of split-second timing when two individual artistic spirits joined together as one. It was an assertion of mutual trust born from long discussions about how best to achieve artistic ends. And it was about the ability to share an implicit trust of one another nurtured over time. Is it too much to suggest that in capturing the essence of such emotions as *Adoration, Tenderness,* or *Joy* through the acting of Marguerite or Eleni that Jim has captured a kind of self portrait that reveals the feminine side of the photographer himself?

At the turn of the century, the Photo-Secessionists sometimes created portraits to suggest emotional states of being. They resorted to a distinct manipulation of film to create a kind of Eden, a sense of otherness that approached images similar to what the French symbolists attempted with words. Edward Steichen's *Thérèse Duncan on the Acropolis* (1921) and William Mortensen's *Fragment of the Black Mass* (1926) serve as two memorable examples whereby gestures of a timeless classic grace and poise expressed by dancers in flowing gowns suggest psychological possibilities that lead the viewer toward a romantic and ethereal world.

Jim Mitchell's images are also about presenting psychological states expressed in poised and meaningful gestures by the mime, actress, or dancer. But Jim's intent is decidedly different. His figures are physically present and up close. In fact they often appear almost as sculpted forms chiseled by heightened shifts between dark and light against a dramatic black background. Rather they call to mind the chiaroscuro techniques favored by painters such as Rembrandt, Tintoretto, and Caravaggio. The viewer's attentions are drawn to accentuated essentials — the voluptuous contours of the female body, the textures that yearn to be touched, and the avoidance of a particular setting. There are no columns of a Greek temple or dewy tree limbs to suggest an exotic other world sometimes favored by the Photo-Secessionists.

Jim's photographs are also about both timelessness and measured time. Most figures are presented "center stage" creating in the viewer a balanced and orderly world associated with the timelessness of rational classicism. As well Jim understands the camera's unique ability to capture time and motion. Indeed the idea of capturing locomotion by a camera capable of taking a series of exposures on a single plate dates back at least to the early 1880's by Etienne Jules Maray in Paris and by Thomas Eakins in Philadelphia. One thinks immediately of the late Berenice Abbott, another photographer-retiree to Maine, who worked single mindedly for nearly two decades to unite art and science through timed exposures of scientific experiments, or of Harold Edgerton's famous bullets-in-flights series in the middle of this century. Jim Mitchell, the career scientist, responds to their visions. Like any truly accomplished artist, Jim has mastered the complex and precise technical demands of his craft so that the results of superimposed images of the female form moving with a rhythmic flourish look deceptively easy.

Most celebrated dancers and dance companies rely on photographs for documentary purposes. Occasionally celebrated photographers turn to the world of dance to explore their own artistic vision. One recalls how popular Martha Graham was among photographers. Edward Steichen was a Graham devotee, and Barbara Morgan in particular photographed and documented Graham and her dancers for many years. Graham's penchant for wrapping herself and her dancers in a wealth of black or white material that extended with the movement made for eye-catching photographs as well as choreography. In *Body & Soul*, Jim Mitchell bypasses dance as documentation to capture essential human emotions through the grace and drama of dance movements. While there is a distinguished precedence for his subject in American photography, Jim Mitchell's voice seems unique in Maine at the present time. His presence among us is all the more welcome for it.

Maine Coast Artists, Rockport, Maine
February, 1999

Intellect is to emotion as our clothes are to our bodies;
we could not very well have civilized life without clothes,
but we would be in a poor way indeed if
we only had clothes without bodies.

ALFRED NORTH WHITEHEAD, 1861-1947

It is the addition of strangeness to beauty that
constitutes the romantic character in art.

WALTER PATER, 1839-1894

Little soul, wandering, gentle guest and companion of the body, into what places will you now go, pale, stiff, and naked, no longer sporting as you did!

HADRIAN, A.D. 76-138

PERFORMED BY ELENI KOENKA
1998

Body and Soul

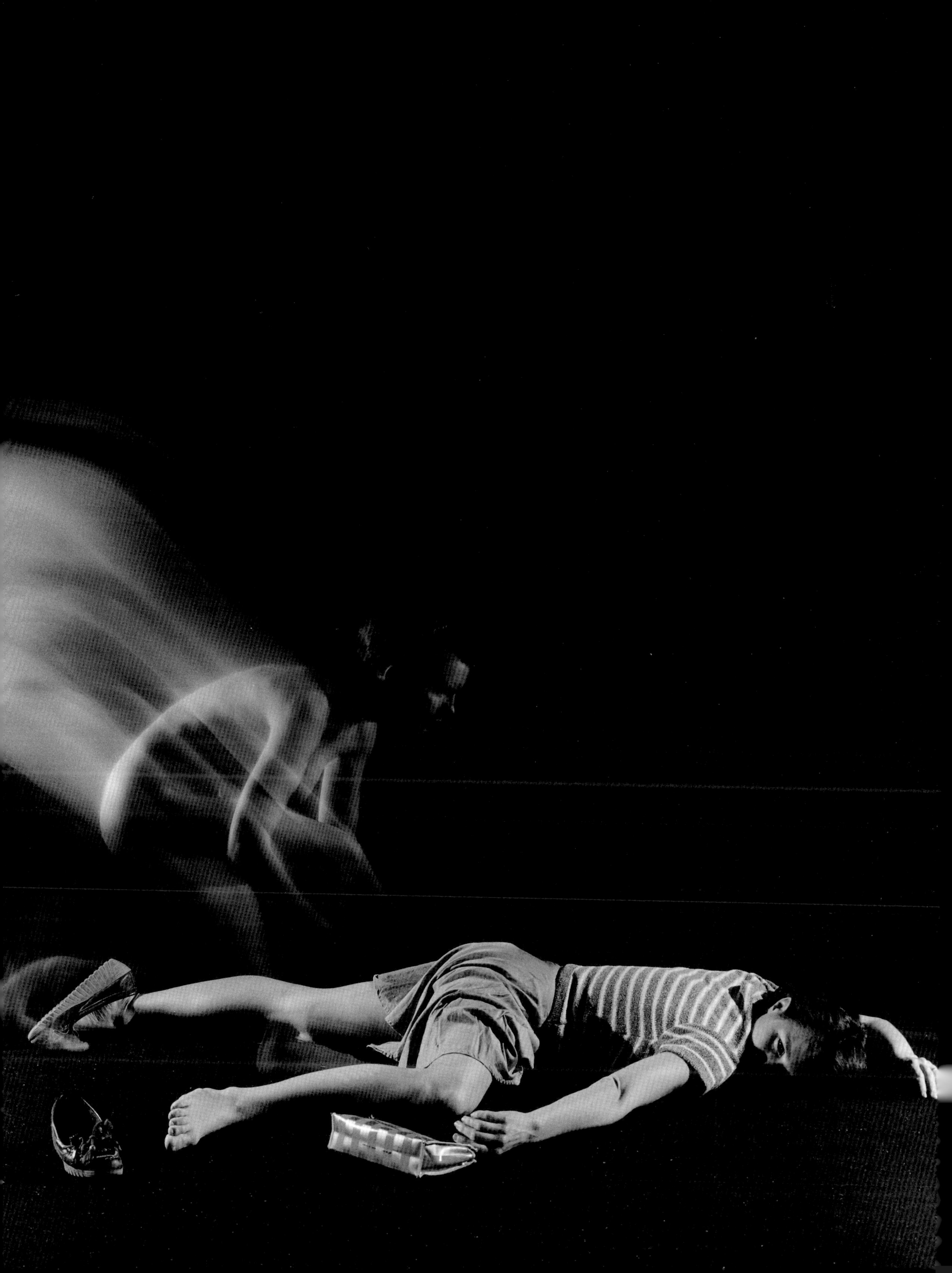

She says, "But in contentment I still feel
The need of some imperishable bliss."
Death is the mother of beauty; hence from her,
Alone, shall come the fulfillment of our dreams
And our desires.

WALLACE STEVENS, 1879-1955
SUNDAY MORNING

PERFORMED BY ELENI KOENKA
1998

Contentment

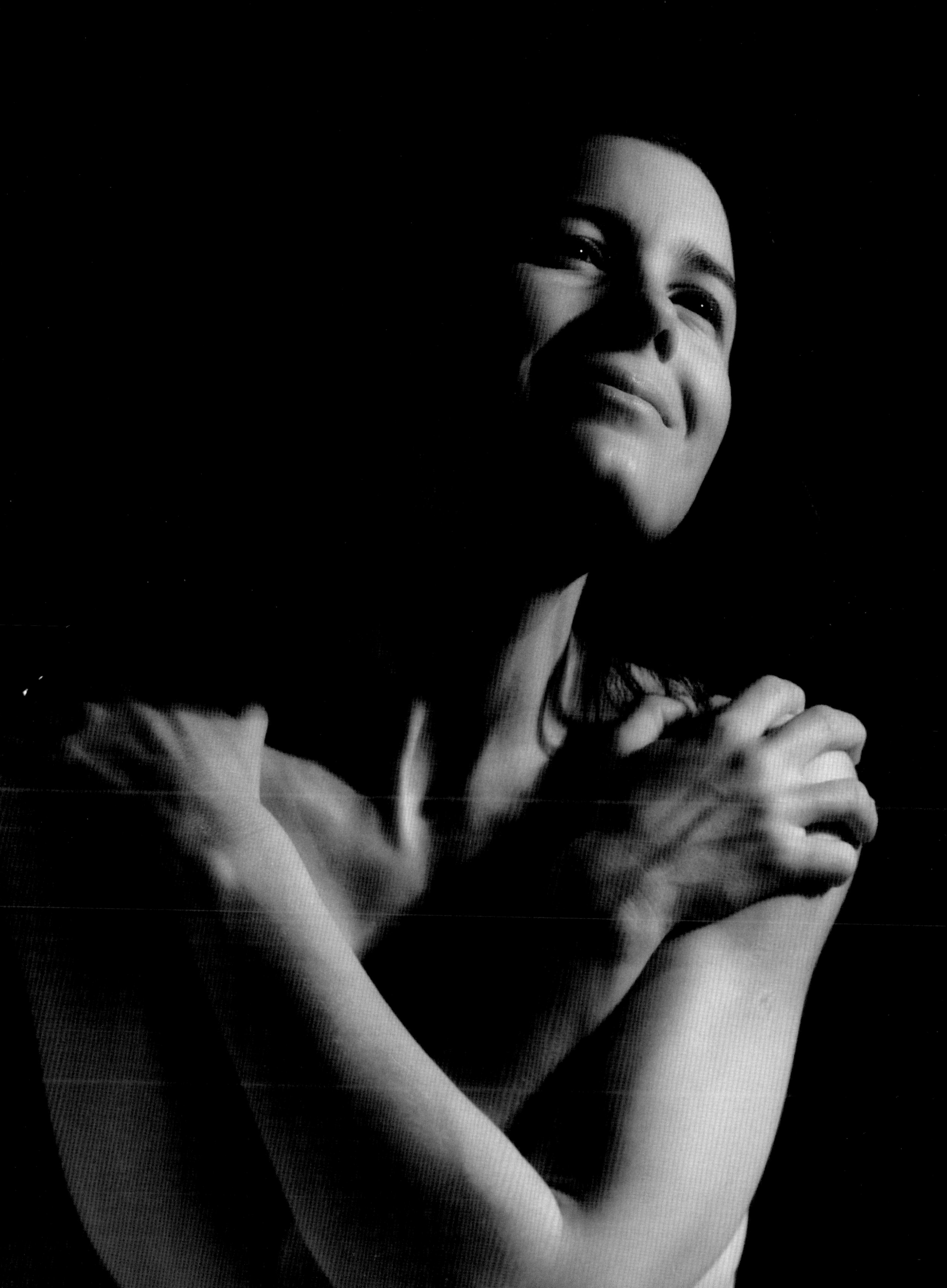

Serene, I fold my hands and wait,
Nor care for wind, nor tide, nor sea;
I rave no more 'gainst time nor fate,
For lo! my own shall come to me.

JOHN BURROUGHS, 1837-1921
WAITING

PERFORMED BY SUSAN ABBOTT
1998

Serenity

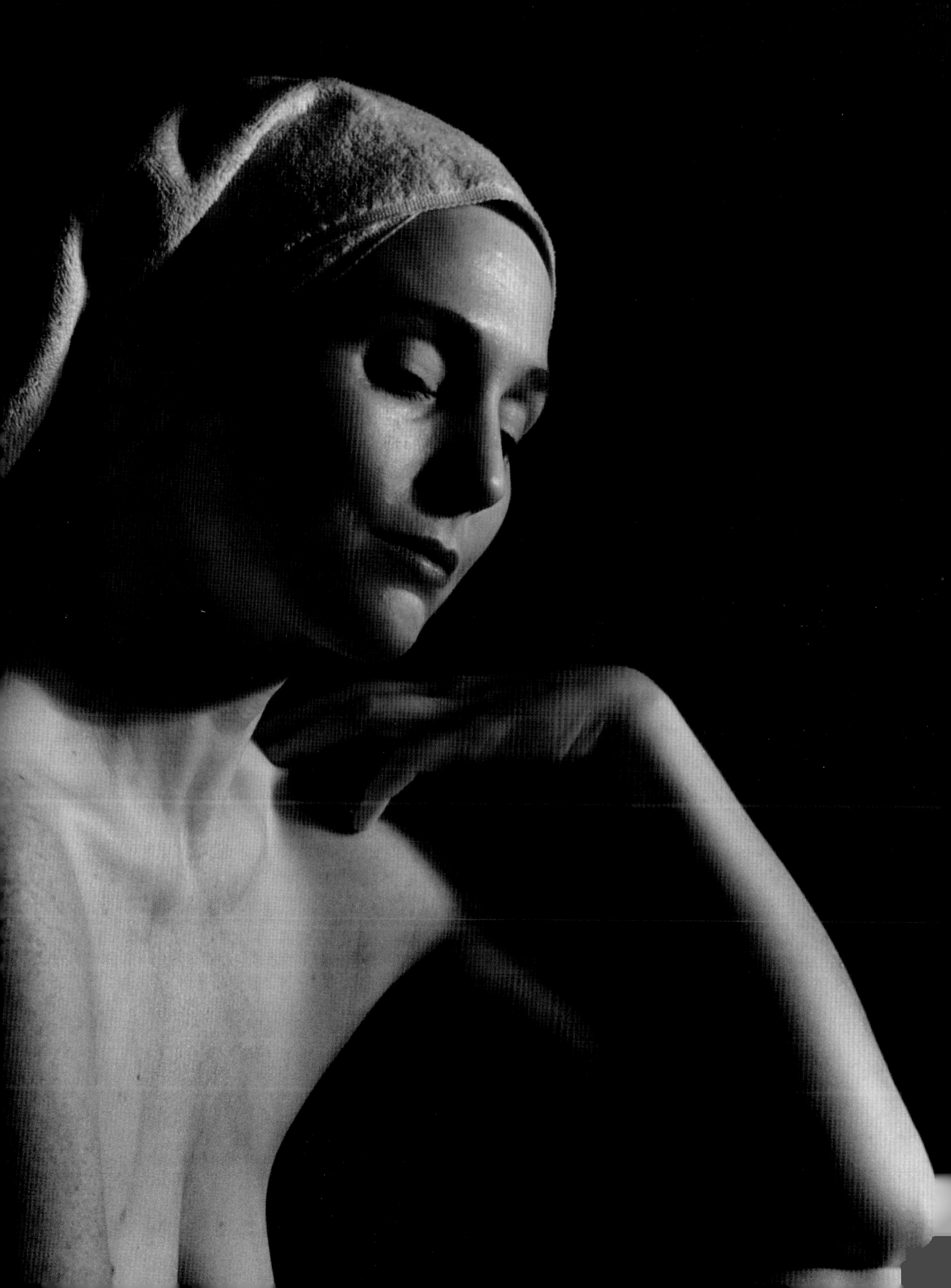

Everything that is exquisite hides itself.

JOSEPH ROUX, 1834-1886

PERFORMED BY ELENI KOENKA

1997

Surprise

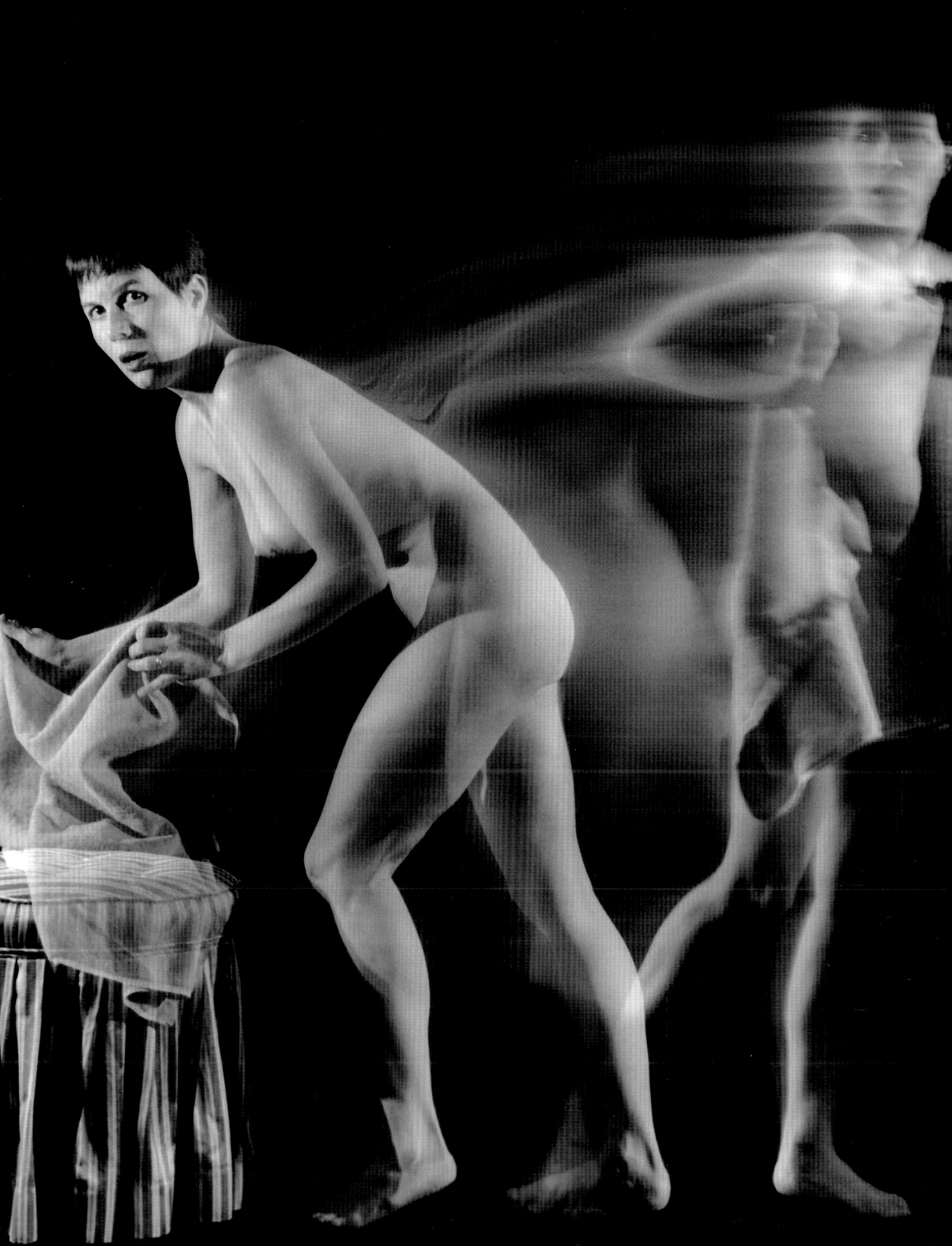

Each of us wears an outer shield,
Armor to protect our vulnerable inner self.

JAMES ANDREW MITCHELL, 1926-

What will you become now?
Everything lives inside its own form
of loneliness —

NORA MITCHELL, 1956-
GNOSIS

PERFORMED BY ELENI KOENKA
1998

Protecting our Inner Self

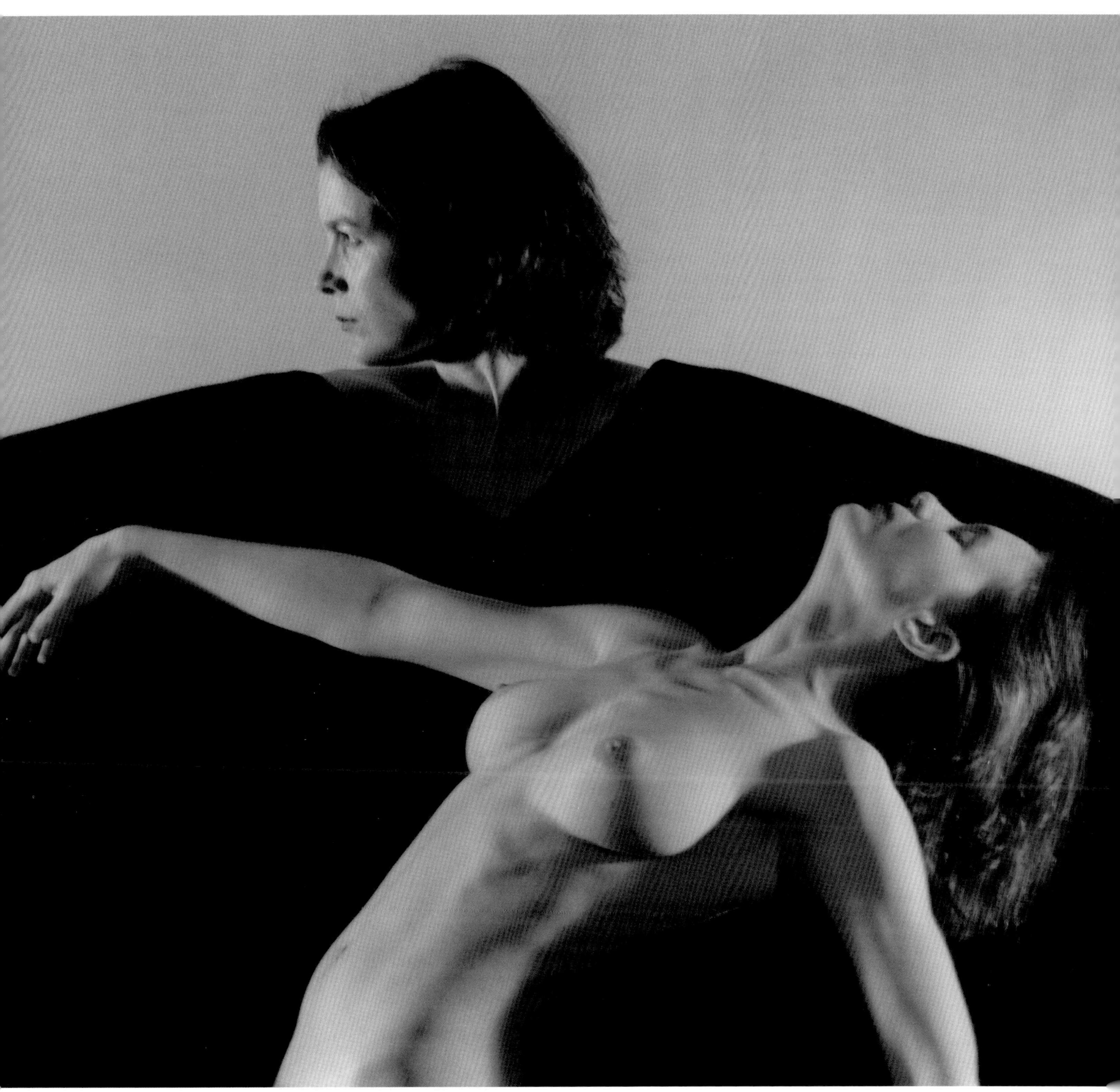

She that respects herself is safe from others;
She wears a coat of mail that none can pierce.

HENRY WADSWORTH LONGFELLOW, 1807-1882

PERFORMED BY ELENI KOENKA
1996

Pride

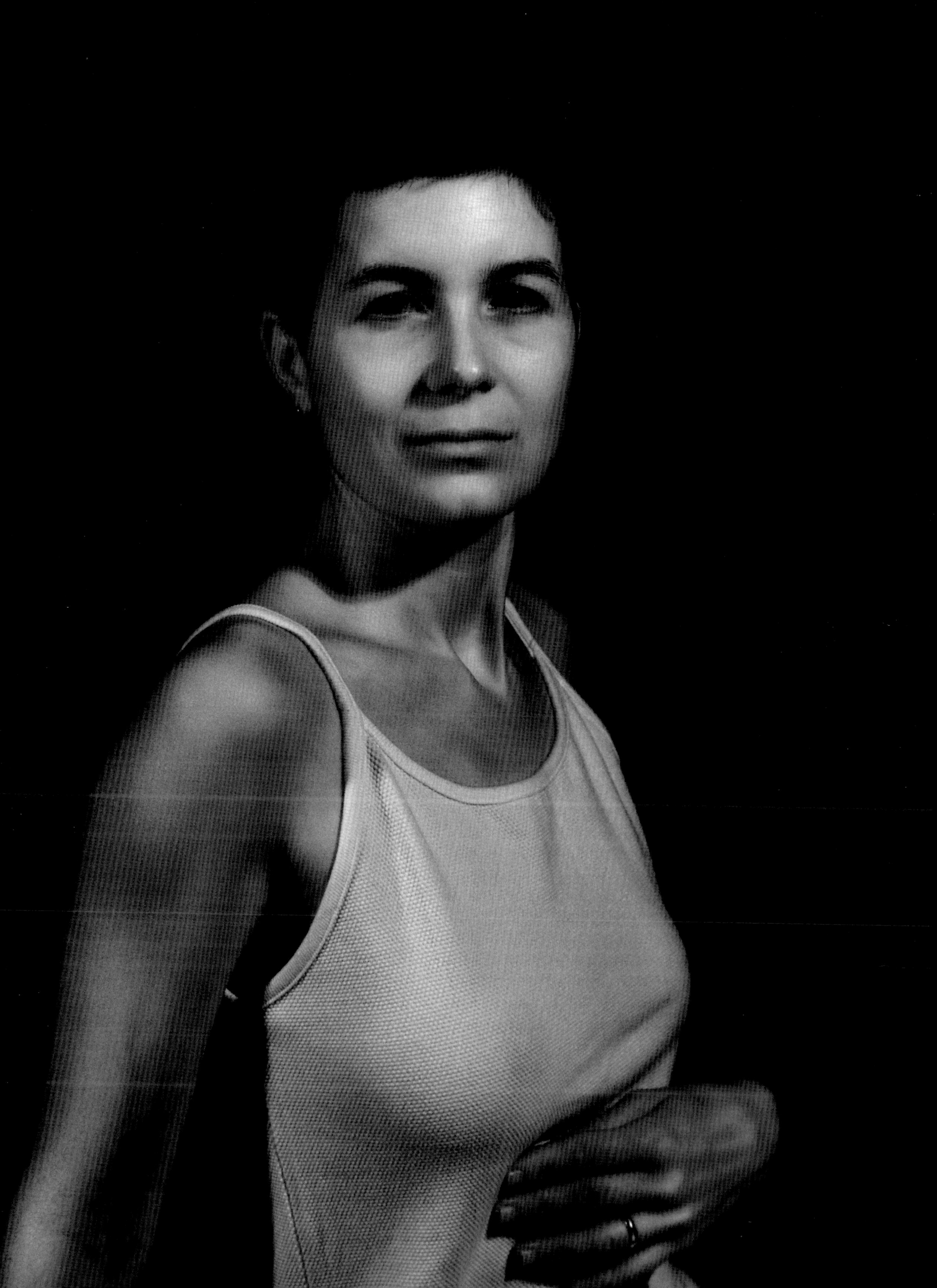

Life does not give itself to one
who tries to keep all its advantages at once.
I have often thought morality may perhaps consist
solely in the courage of making a choice.

LEON BLUM, 1872-1950
ON MARRIAGE

PERFORMED BY SUSAN ABBOTT
1998

Choice

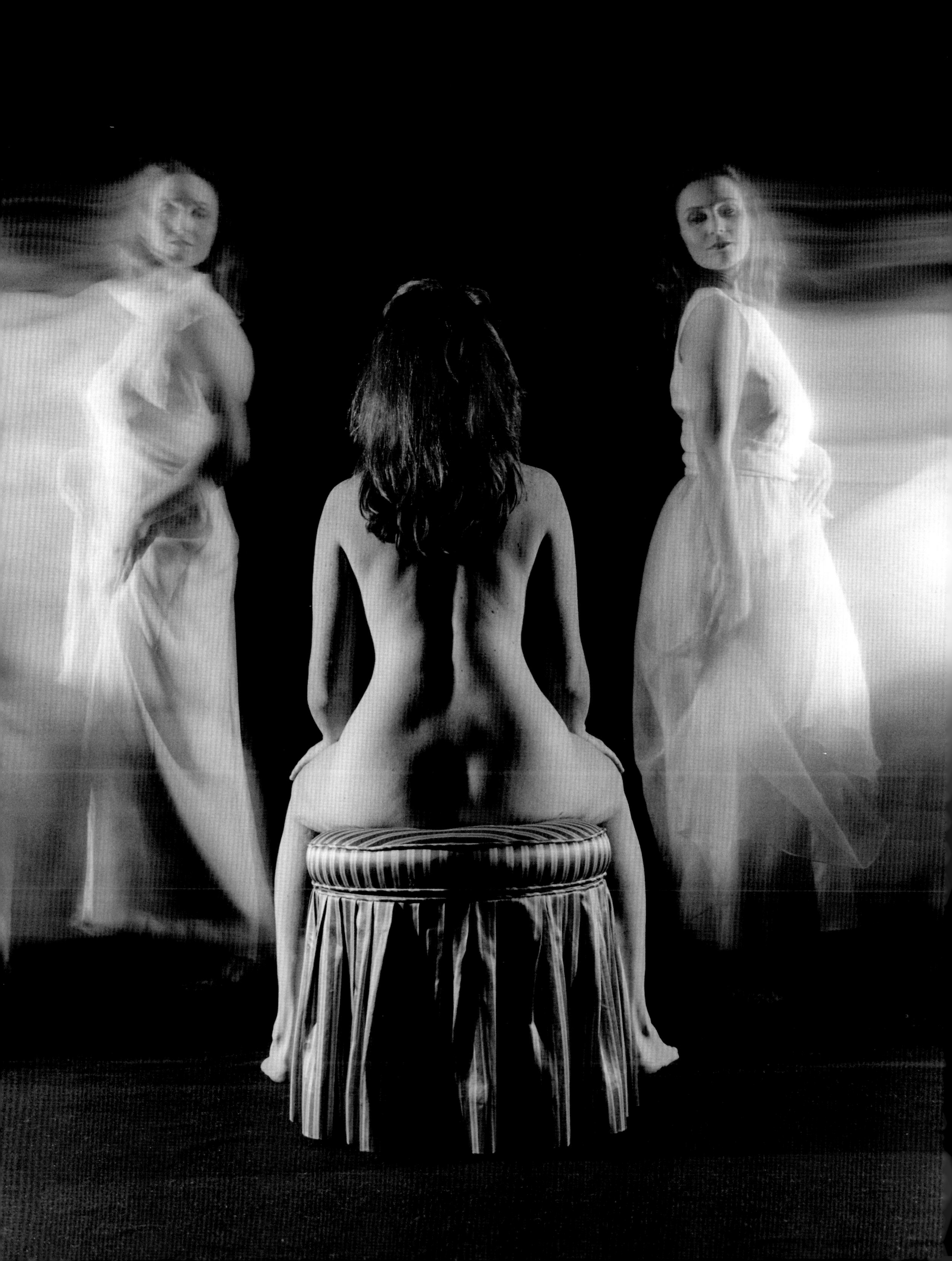

To jump with wild abandon into the river of life requires not only exuberance, but great confidence in one's own self!

JAMES ANDREW MITCHELL, 1926-

PERFORMED BY ELENI KOENKA
1997

Abandon

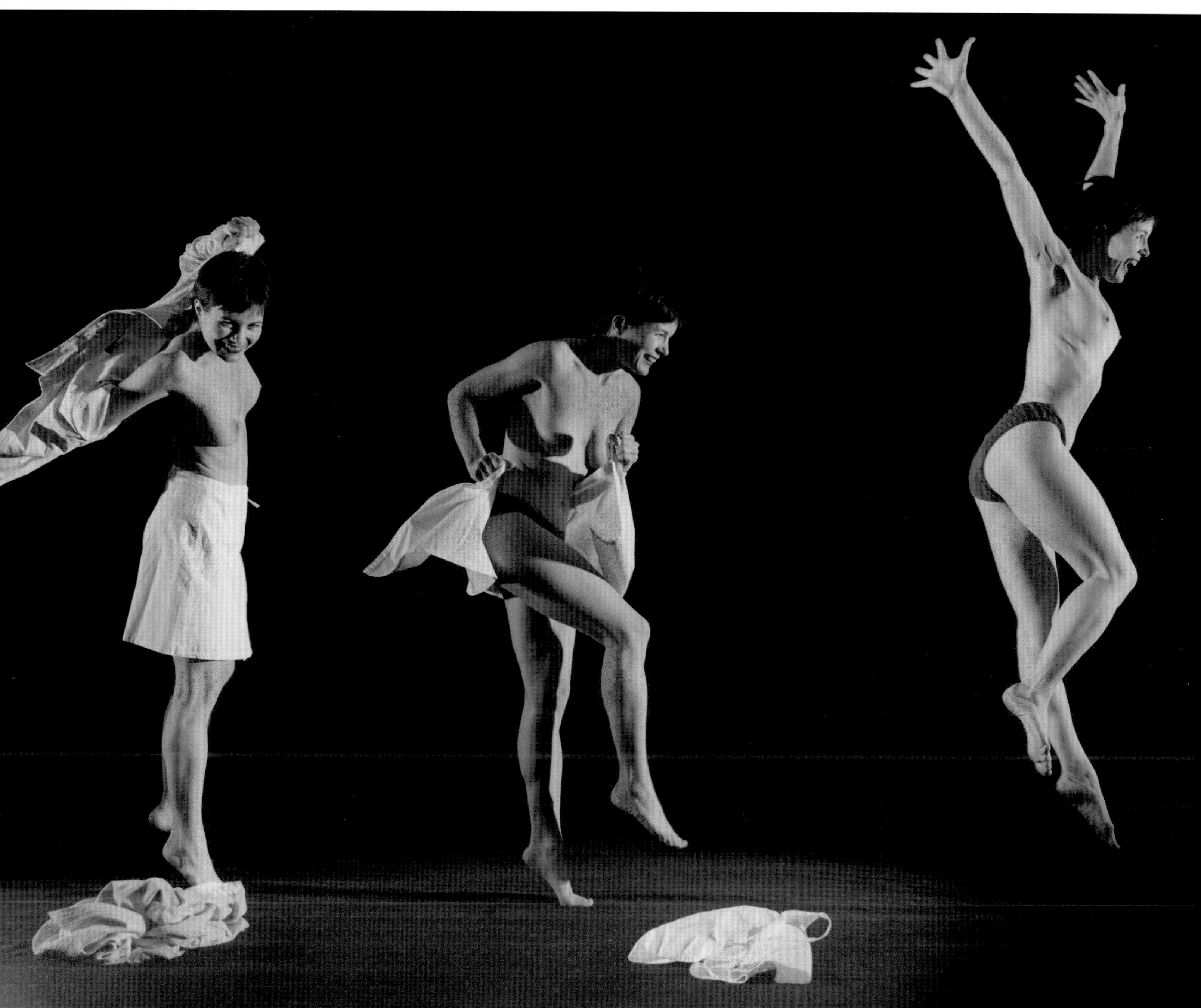

On with the dance! Let Joy be unconcerned;
No sleep till morn, when Youth and Pleasure meet
To chase the glowing hours with flying feet.

LORD BYRON, 1788-1824

PERFORMED BY ELENI KOENKA
1997

Joy

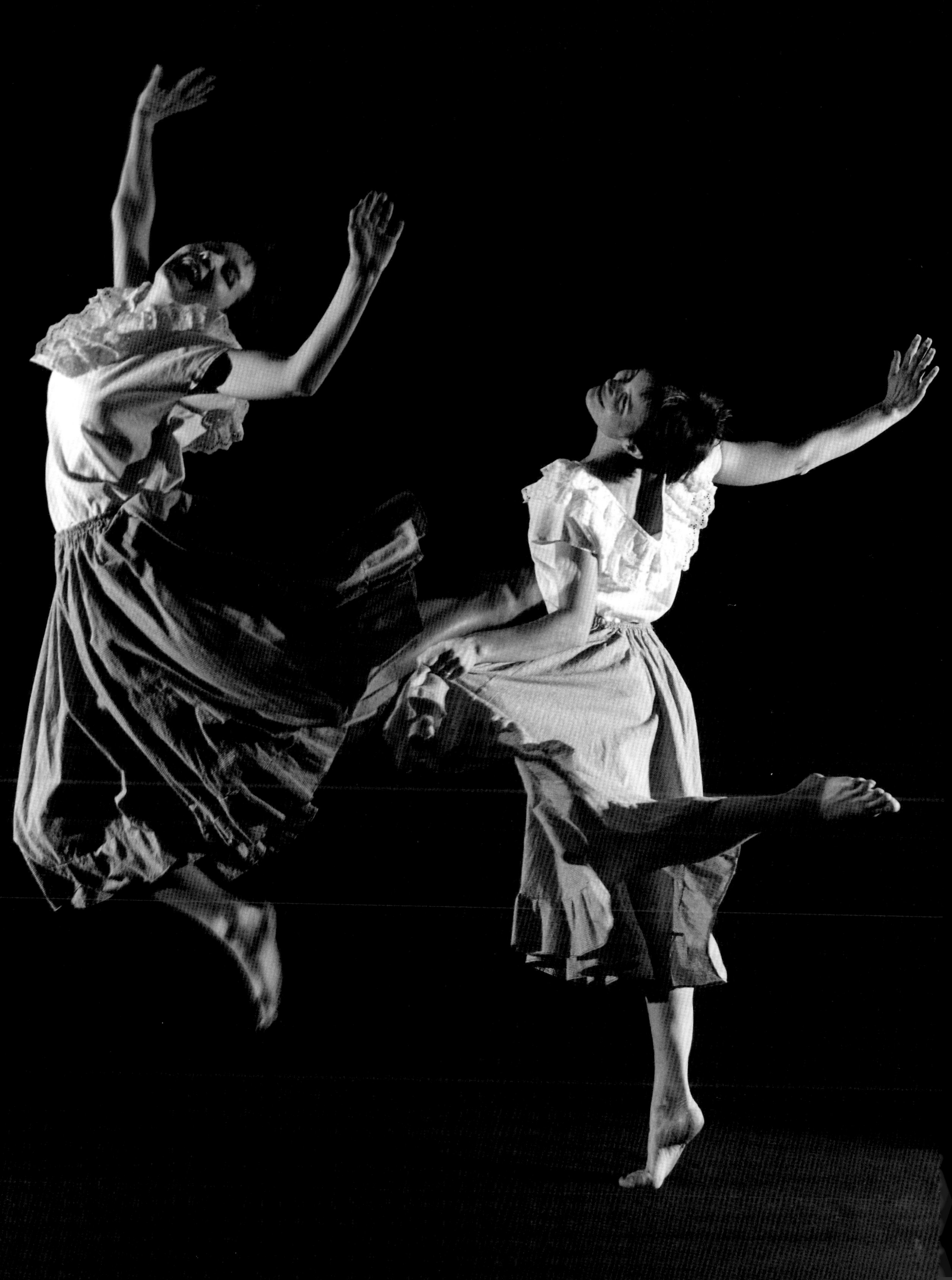

— naked, unshy, beautiful, and full of grace —

JOHN CHEEVER, 1912-1982
GOODBYE MY BROTHER

PERFORMED BY ELENI KOENKA
1997

Grace

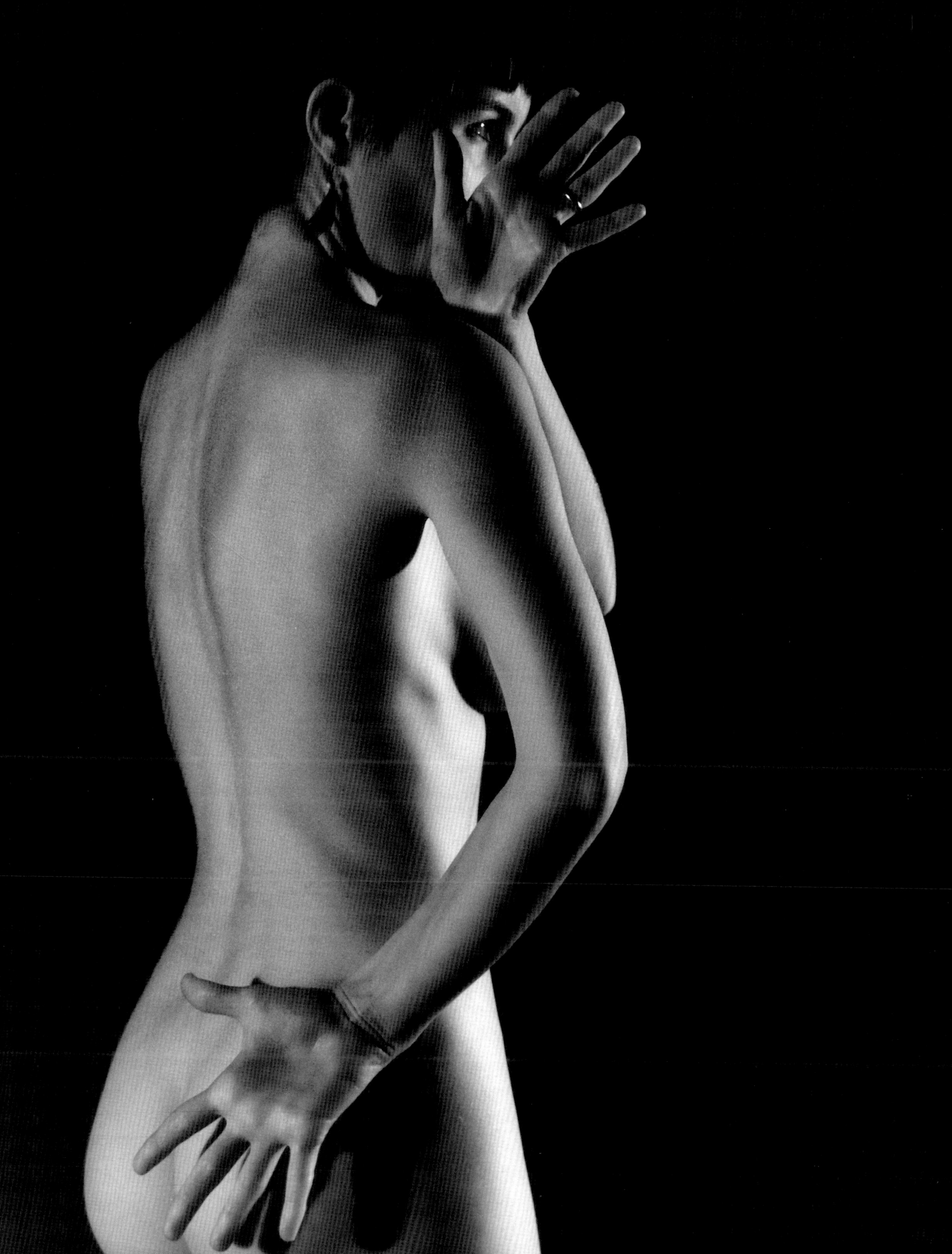

Oh, what a dear ravishing thing is the beginning of an Amour!

(MRS) APHRA BEHN, 1640-1689
THE EMPEROR OF THE MOON

PERFORMED BY SUSAN ABBOTT
1998

Seduction

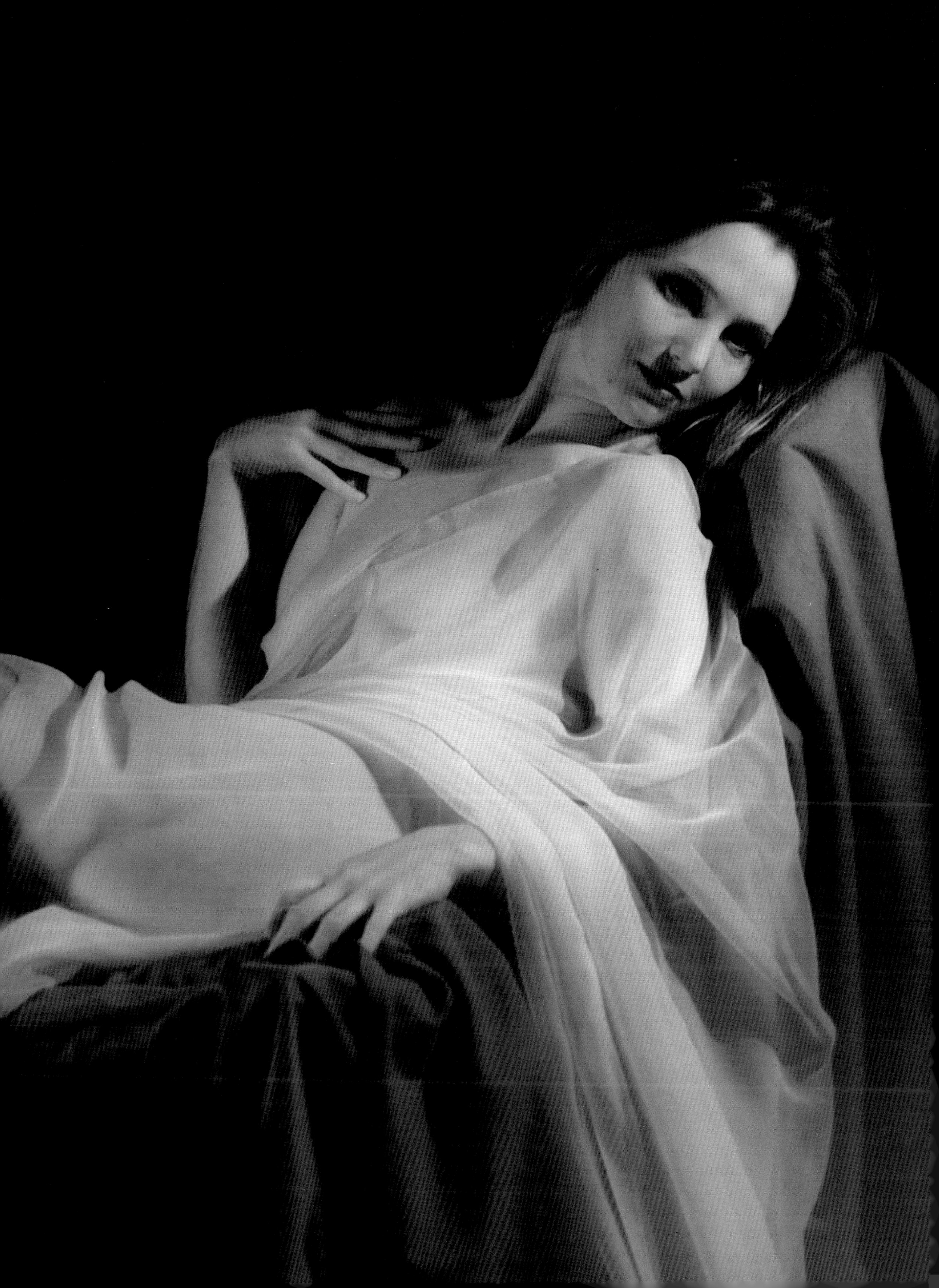

Misled by fancy's meteor ray
By passion driven;
But yet the light that led astray
Was light from heaven.

ROBERT BURNS, 1759-1796
THE VISION

PERFORMED BY ELENI AND DAVID KOENKA
1997

Passion

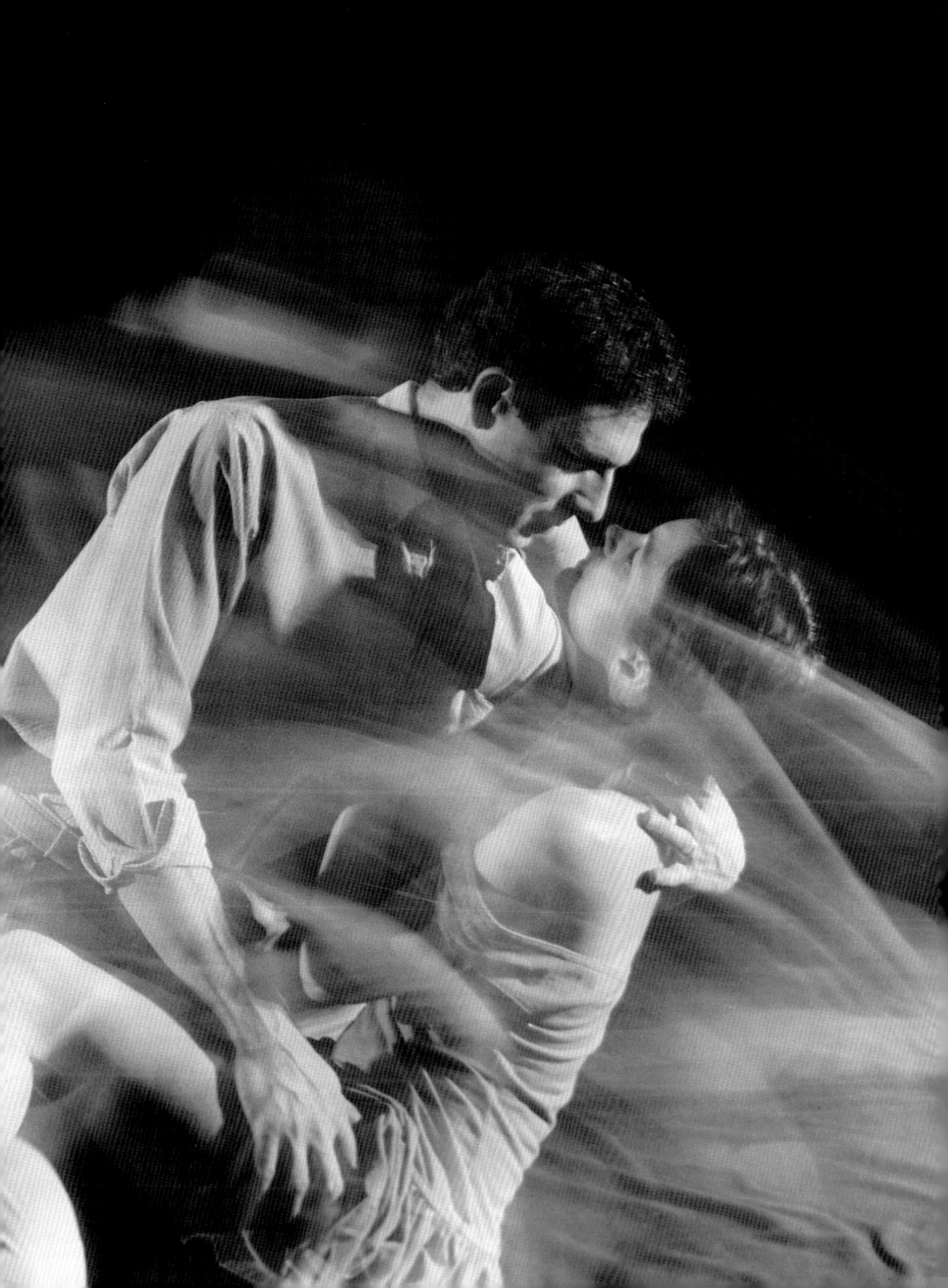

She who ne'er answers till a husband cools,
Or, if she rules him, never shows she rules;
Charms by accepting, by submitting, sways,
Yet has her humor most, when she obeys.

JOHN MILTON, 1608-1674

PERFORMED BY MARGUERITE MATHEWS
1992

Submission

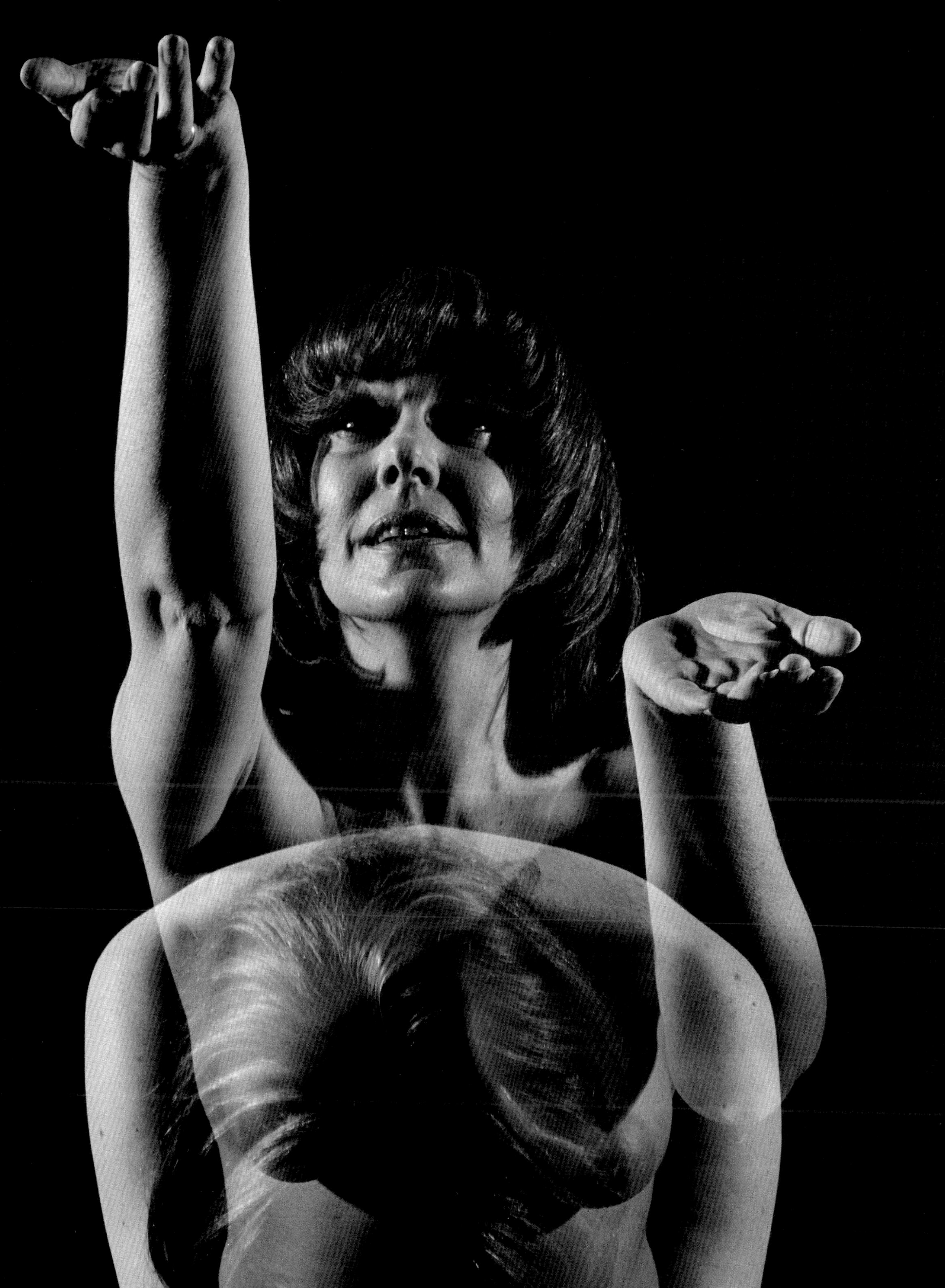

Down in adoration falling,
Lo! the sacred Host we hail;
Lo! o'r ancient forms departing,
Newer rites of grace prevail;
Faith for all defects supplying,
Where the feeble senses fail.

SAINT THOMAS AQUINAS, C. 1225-1274

PERFORMED BY MARGUERITE MATHEWS
1992

Adoration

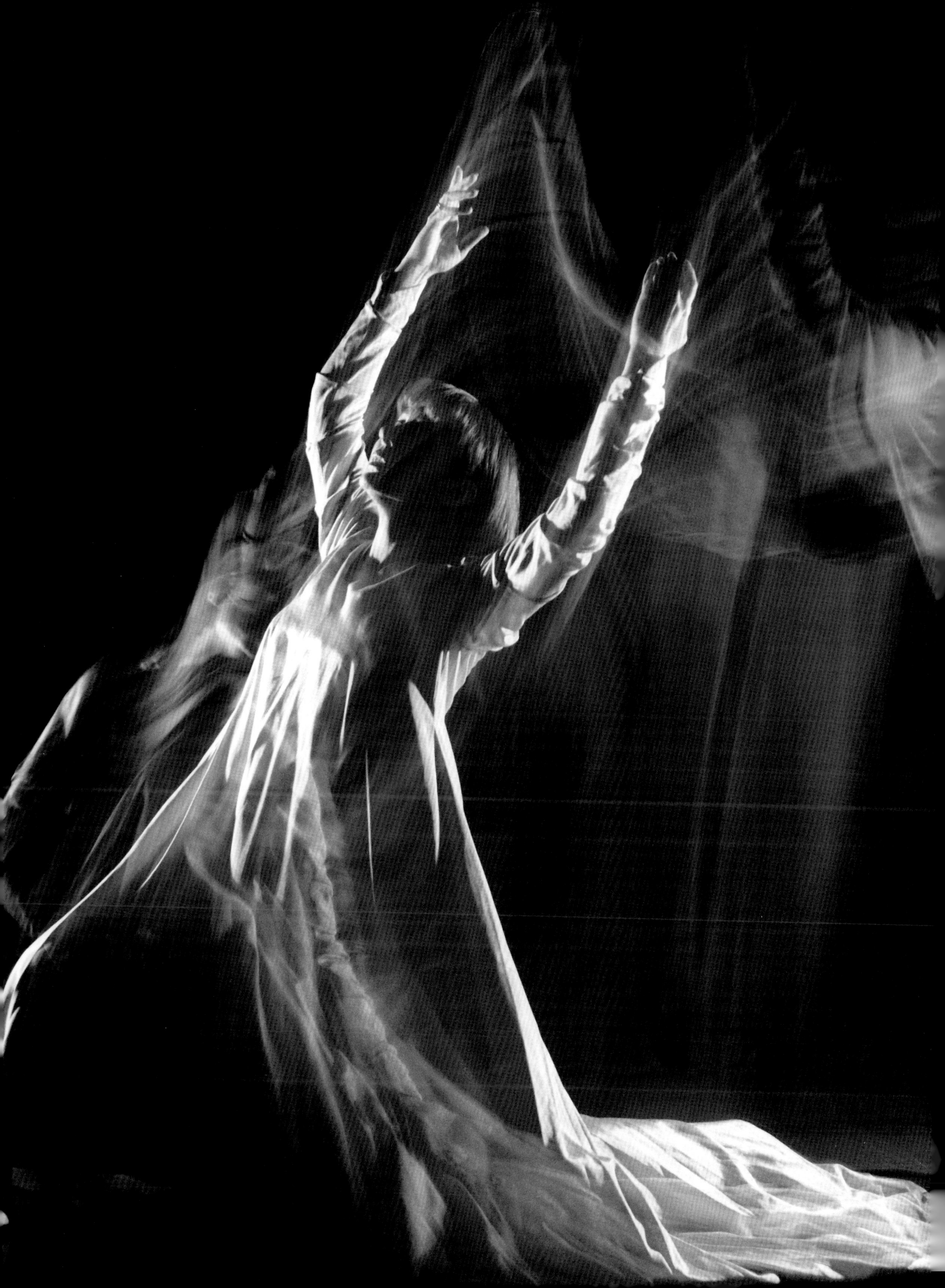

I burned my life, that I might find
A passion wholly of the mind,
Thought divorced from eye and bone,
Ecstasy come to breath alone.

LOUISE BOGAN, 1897-1970
THE ALCHEMIST

PERFORMED BY SUSAN ABBOTT
1998

Ecstasy

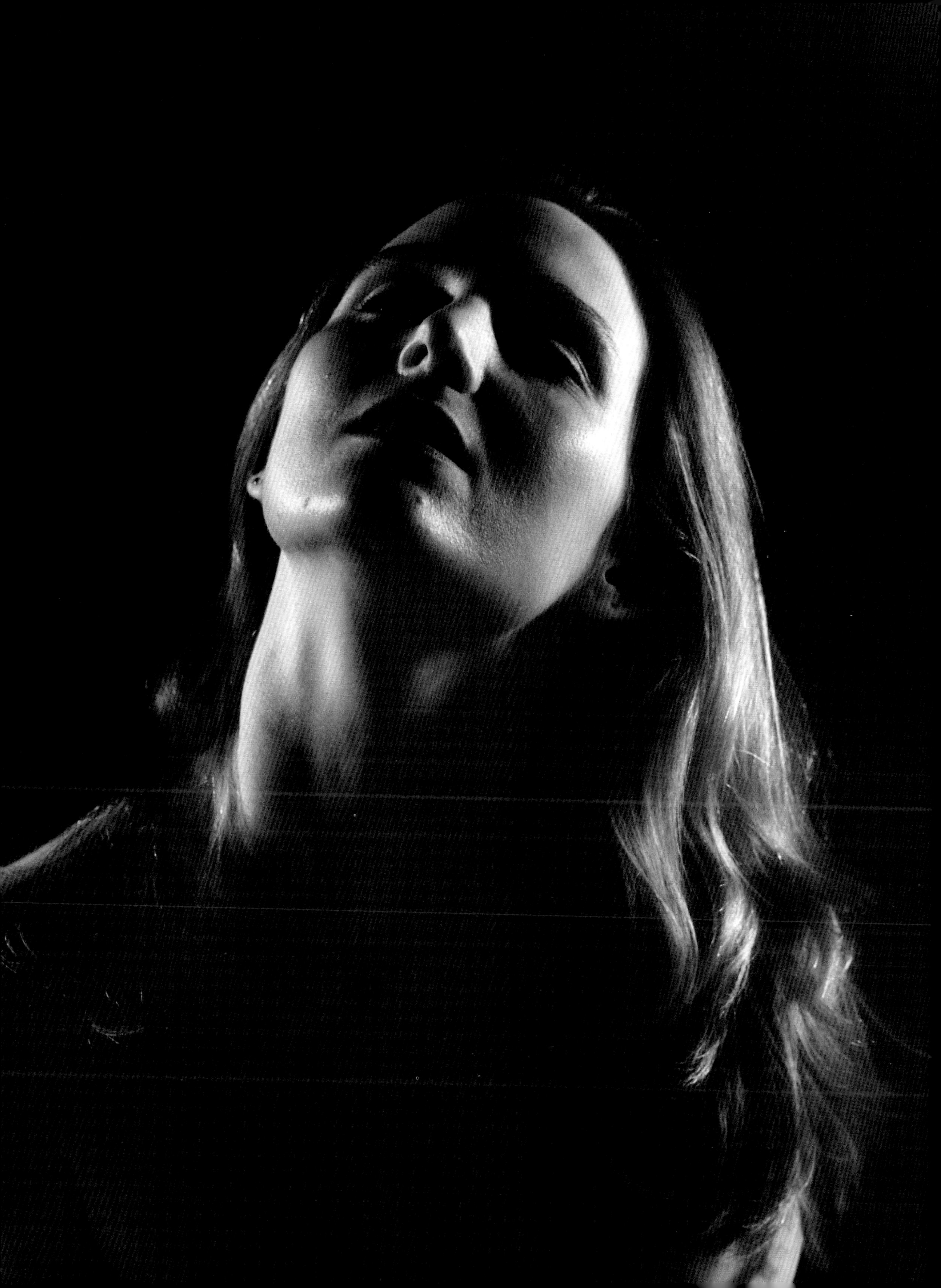

*Beware of allowing a tactless word, a rebuttal,
a rejection to obliterate the whole sky.*

CONFUCIOUS, 551-479 B.C. (ATTRIBUTED)

PERFORMED BY ELENI KOENKA
1998

Rejection

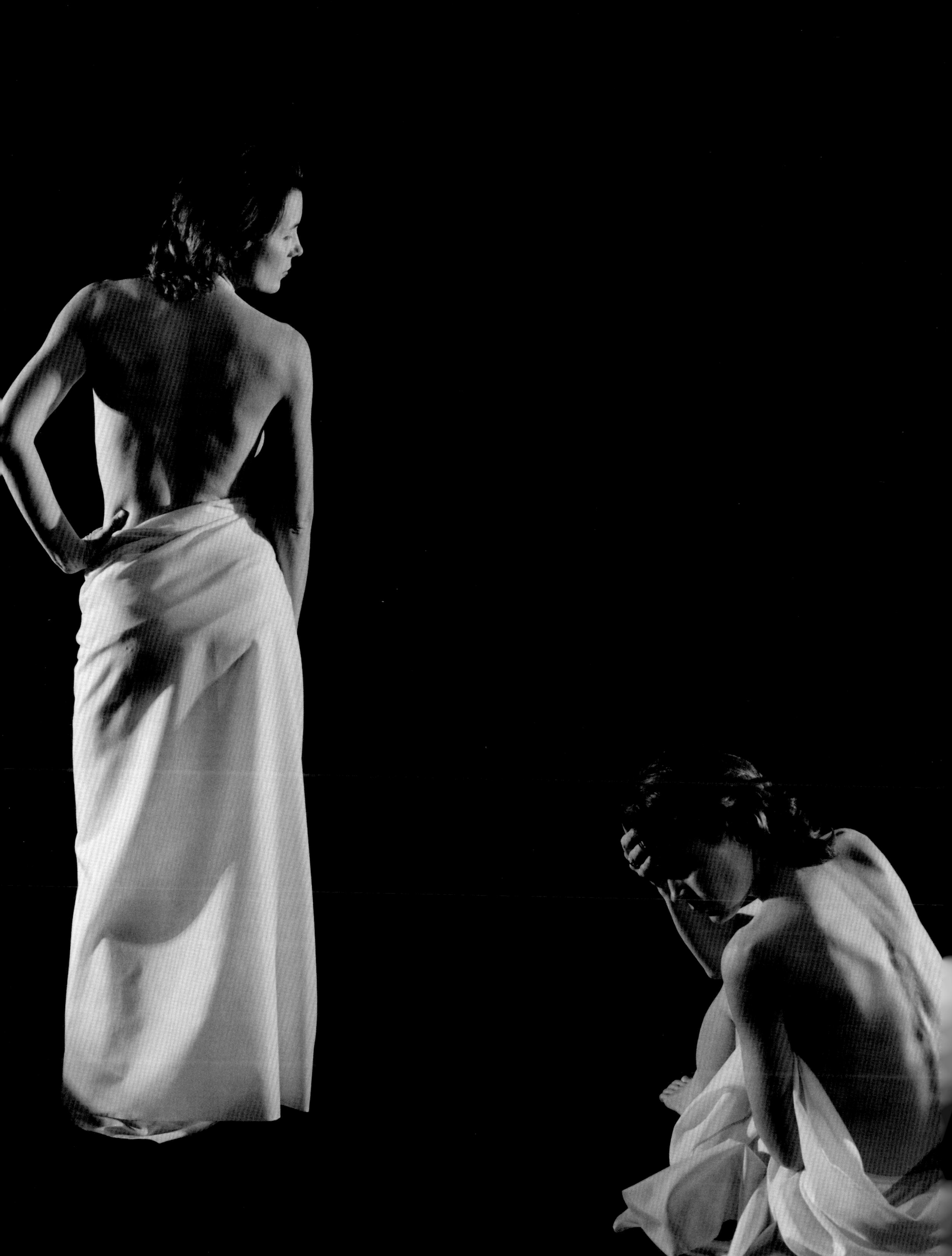

In the life of each of us, I said to myself, there is a place remote and islanded, and given to endless regret or secret happiness.

SARAH ORNE JEWETT, 1849-1909
THE COUNTRY OF THE POINTED FIRS

PERFORMED BY ELENI KOENKA
1998

Regret

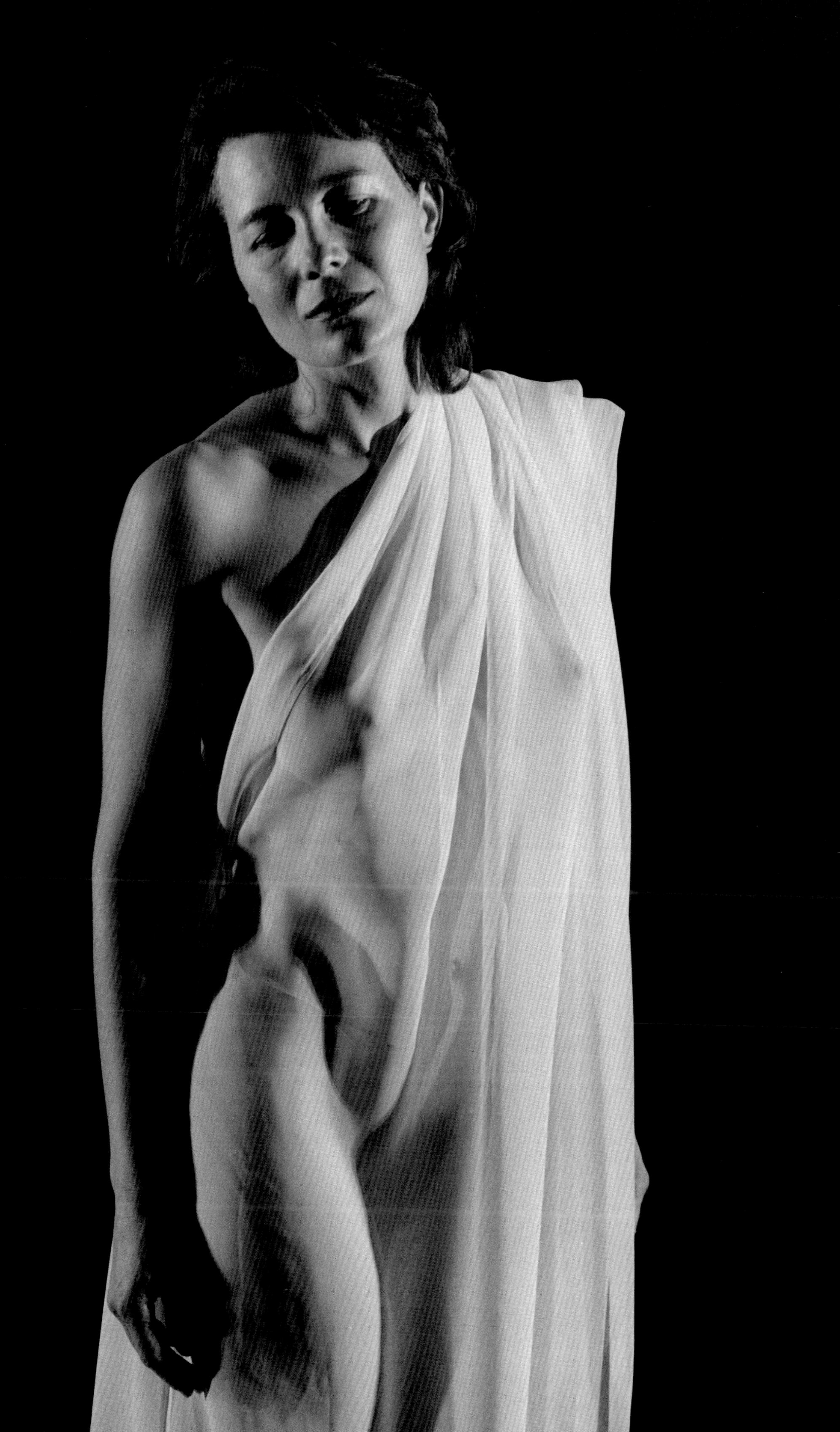

Hence all you vain delights,
As short as are the nights
Wherein you spend your folly!
There's naught in this life sweet
But only melancholy;
O sweetest melancholy!

JOHN FLETCHER, 1579-1625
THE NICE VALOR

PERFORMED BY ELENI KOENKA
1998

Melancholy

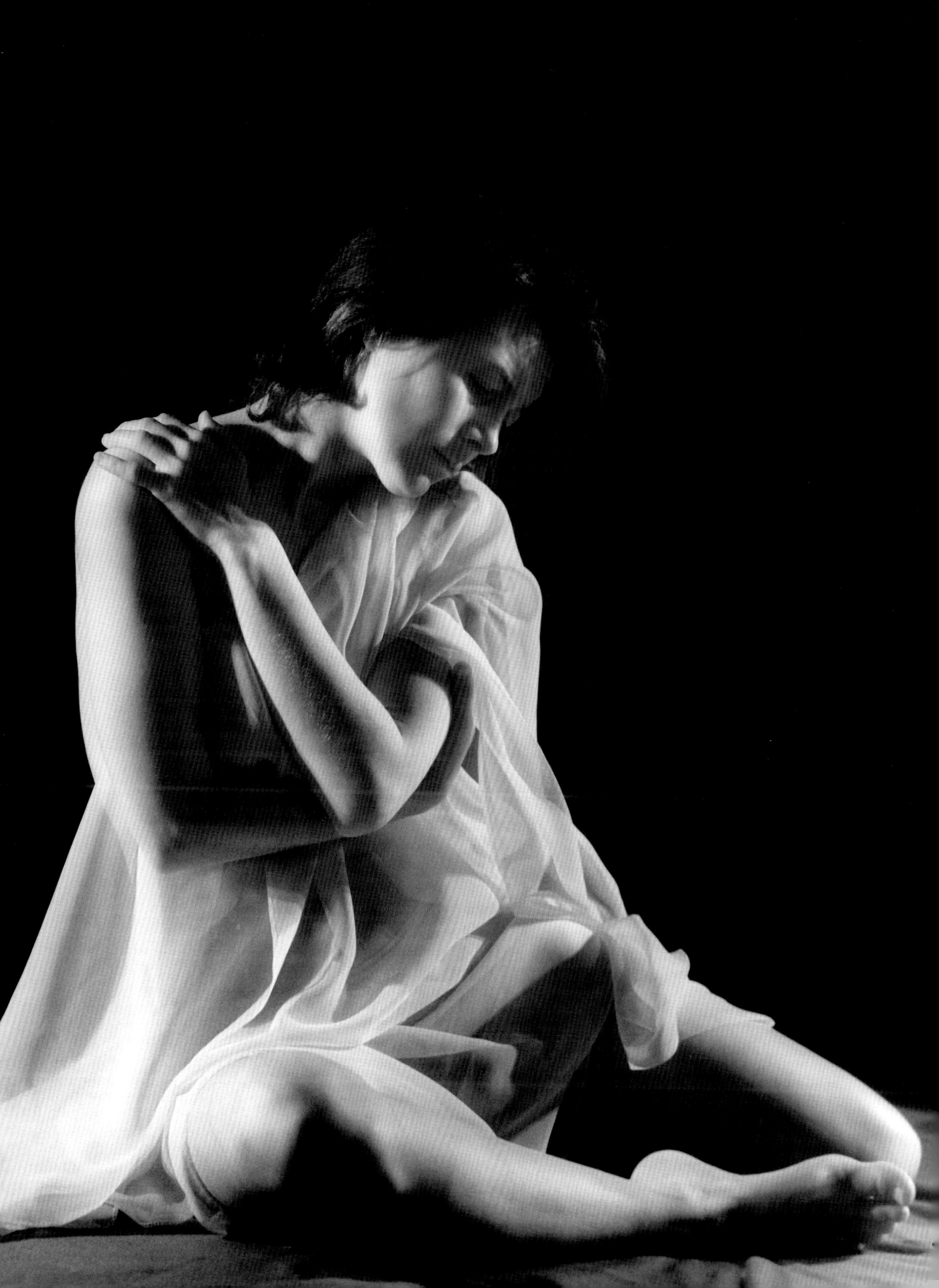

Her nose should part and her lip should curl,
Her cheeks should flame and her brow should furl,
Her bosom should heave and her heart should glow,
And her fist be ever ready for a knockdown blow.

SIR W. S. GILBERT, 1836-1911
(ADAPTED FOR THE FEMININE GENDER)

PERFORMED BY ANNE SAUVÉ
1992

Anger

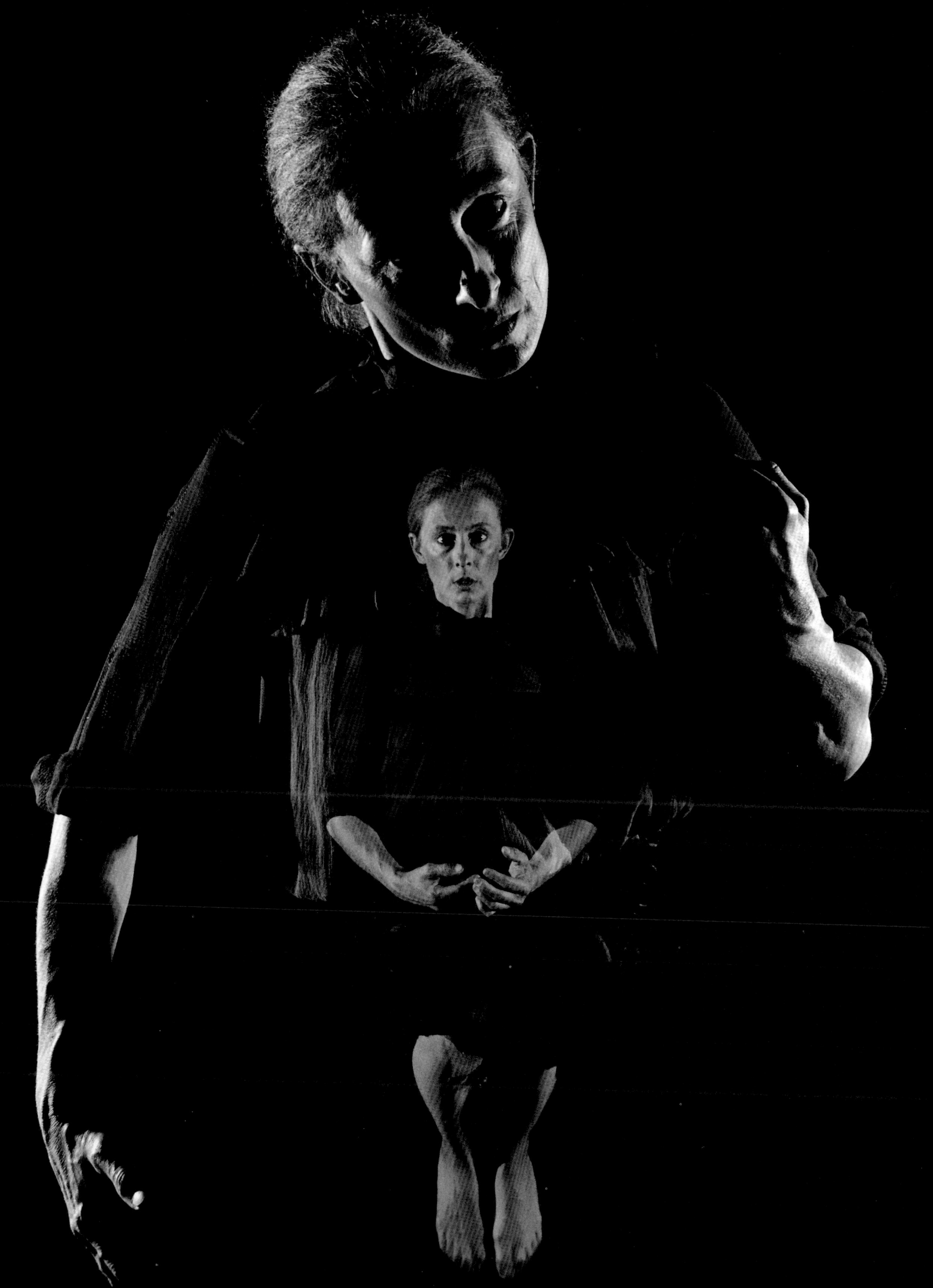

There are glances of hatred that stab and raise no cry of murder.

GEORGE ELIOT, 1819-1880

PERFORMED BY ELENI KOENKA
1997

Hate

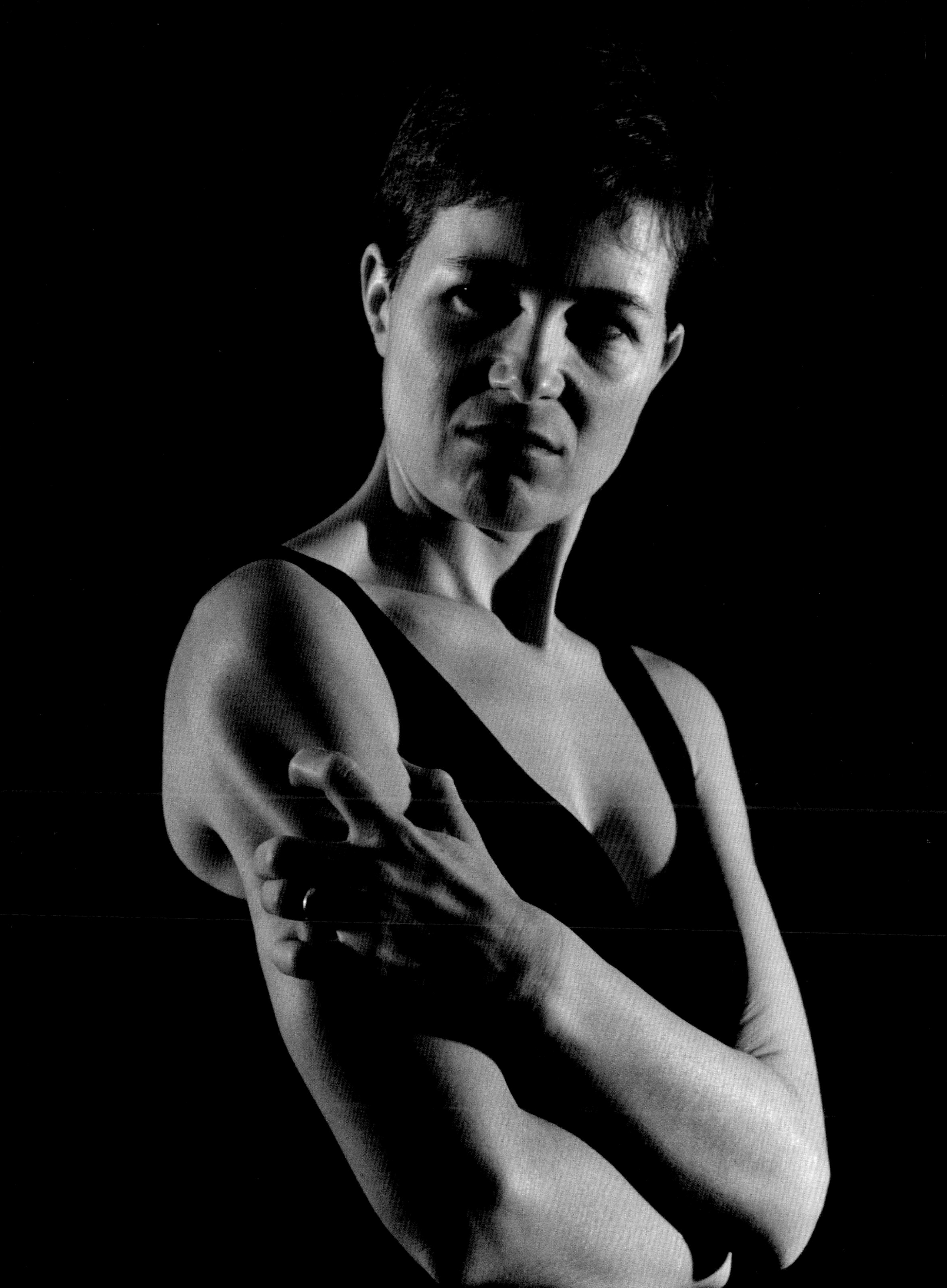

Extreme fear can neither fight nor fly,
But coward-like with trembling terror die.

WILLIAM SHAKESPEARE, 1564-1616
THE RAPE OF LUCRECE

PERFORMED BY ELENI KOENKA
1997

Fear

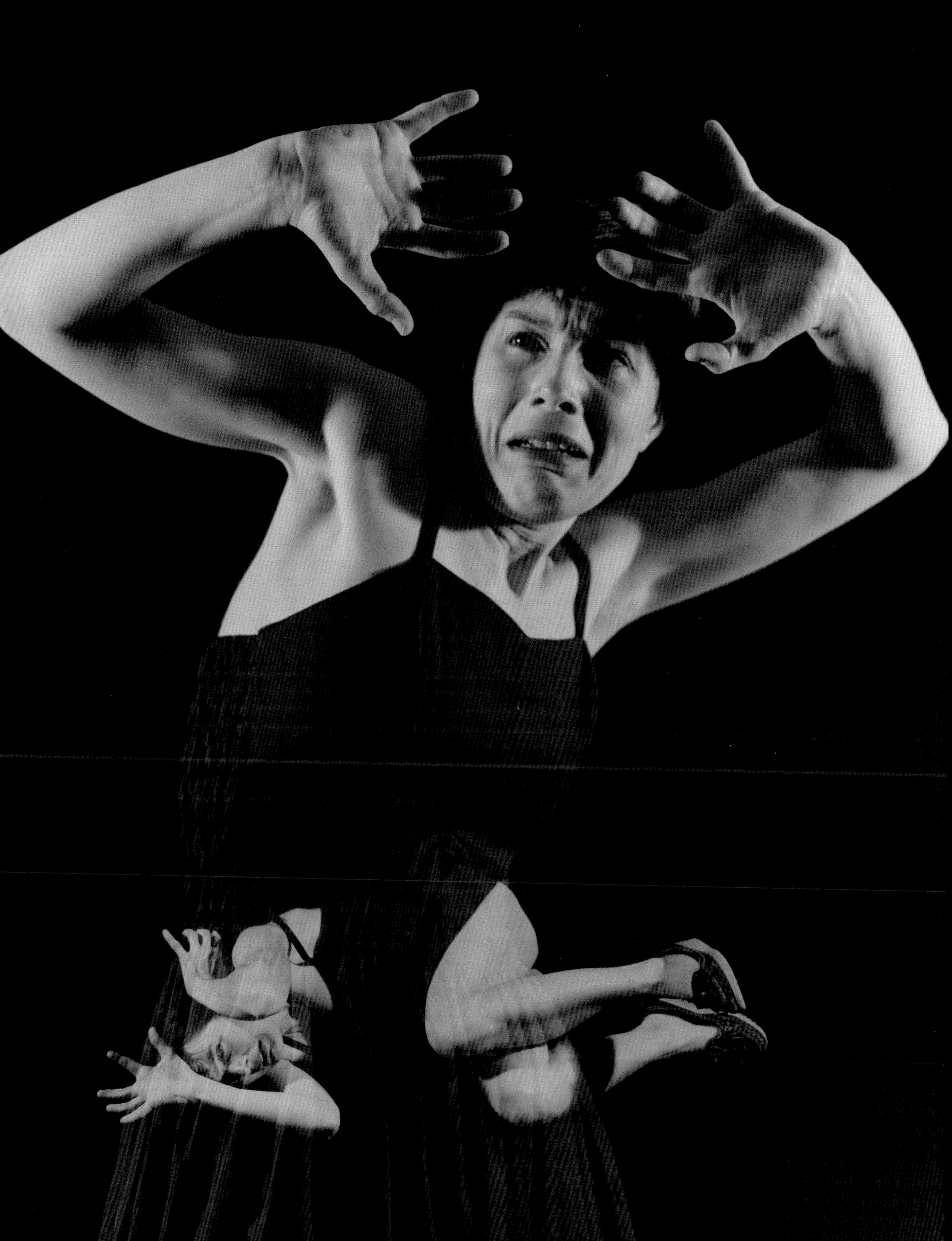

The scarlet letter was her passport
into regions where other women
dared not tread. Shame, Despair,
Solitude! These had been her teachers —
stern and wild ones — and they had made
her strong, but taught her much amiss.

NATHANIEL HAWTHORNE, 1805-1865
THE SCARLET LETTER

PERFORMED BY MARGUERITE MATHEWS
1992

Shame, Despair, Solitude

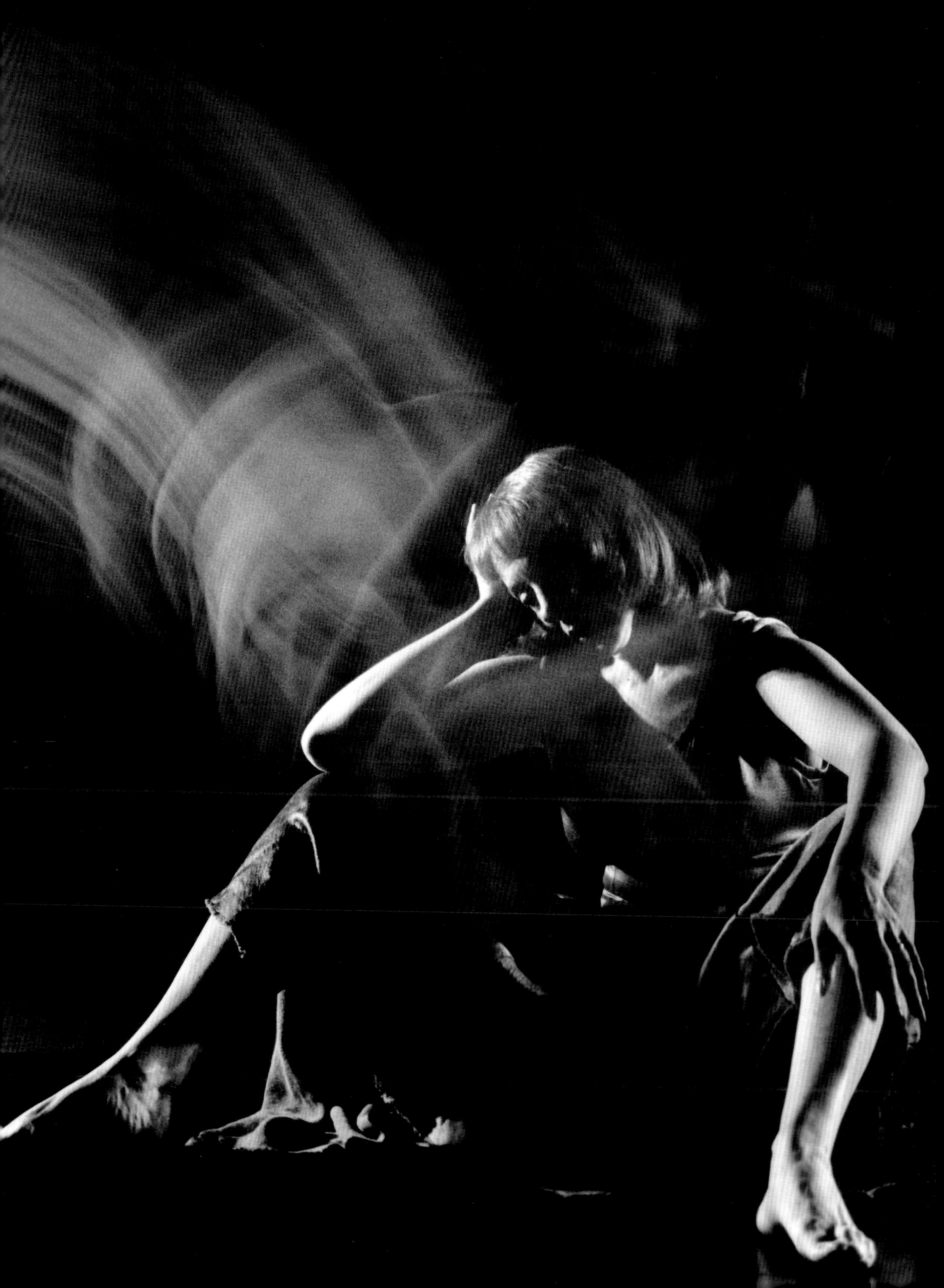

Is there no pity sitting in the clouds,
That sees into the bottom of my grief?

WILLIAM SHAKESPEARE, 1564-1616
ROMEO AND JULIET, ACT III

PERFORMED BY MARGUERITE MATHEWS
1992

Grief

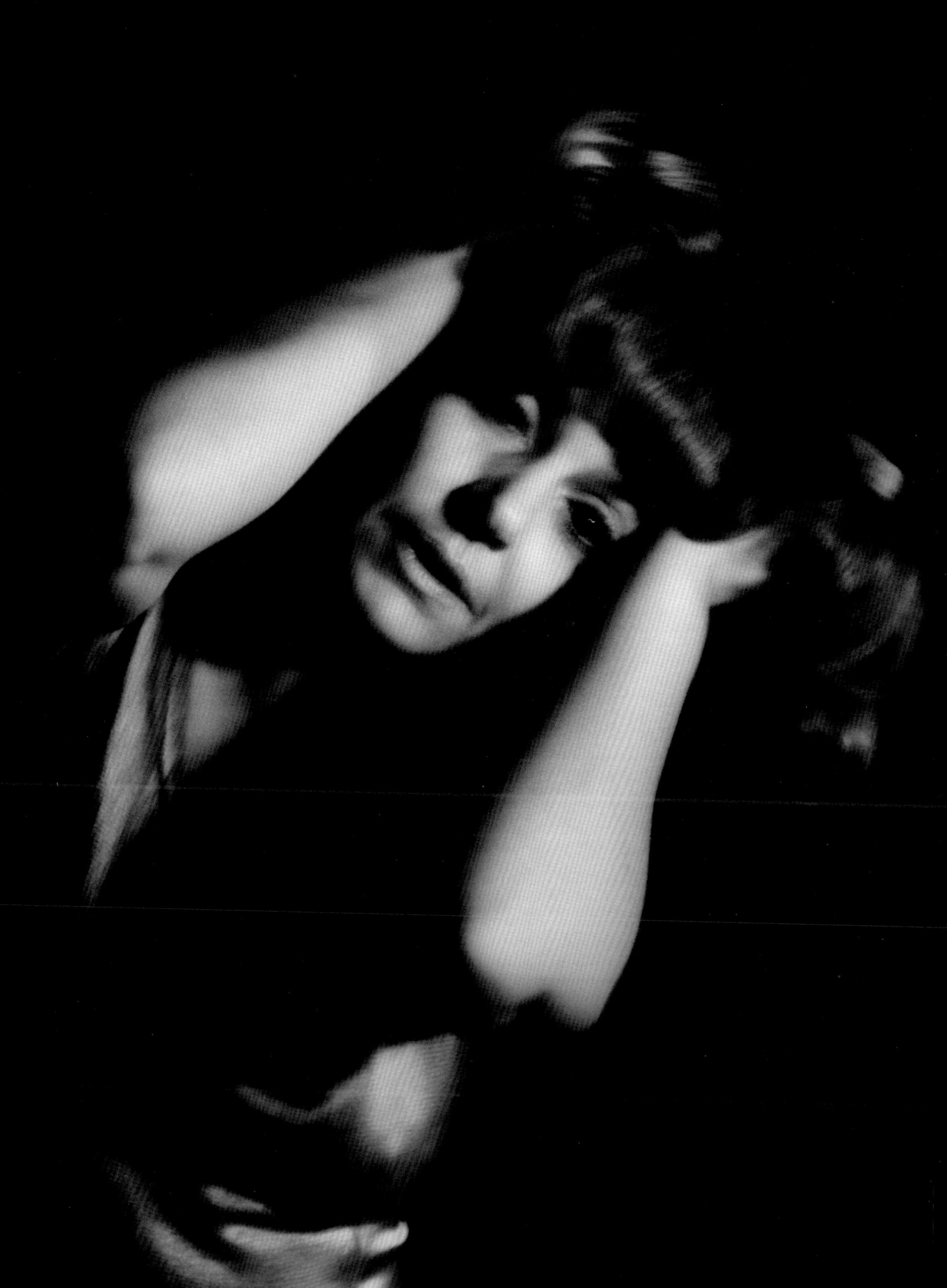

Much madness is divinest Sense —
To a discerning Eye —
Much sense — the starkest Madness
'Tis the Majority
In this, as All, prevail —
Assent — and you are sane —
Demur — you're straightway dangerous —
And handled with a Chain.

EMILY DICKINSON, 1830-1886

PERFORMED BY ANNE SAUVÉ
1992

Madness

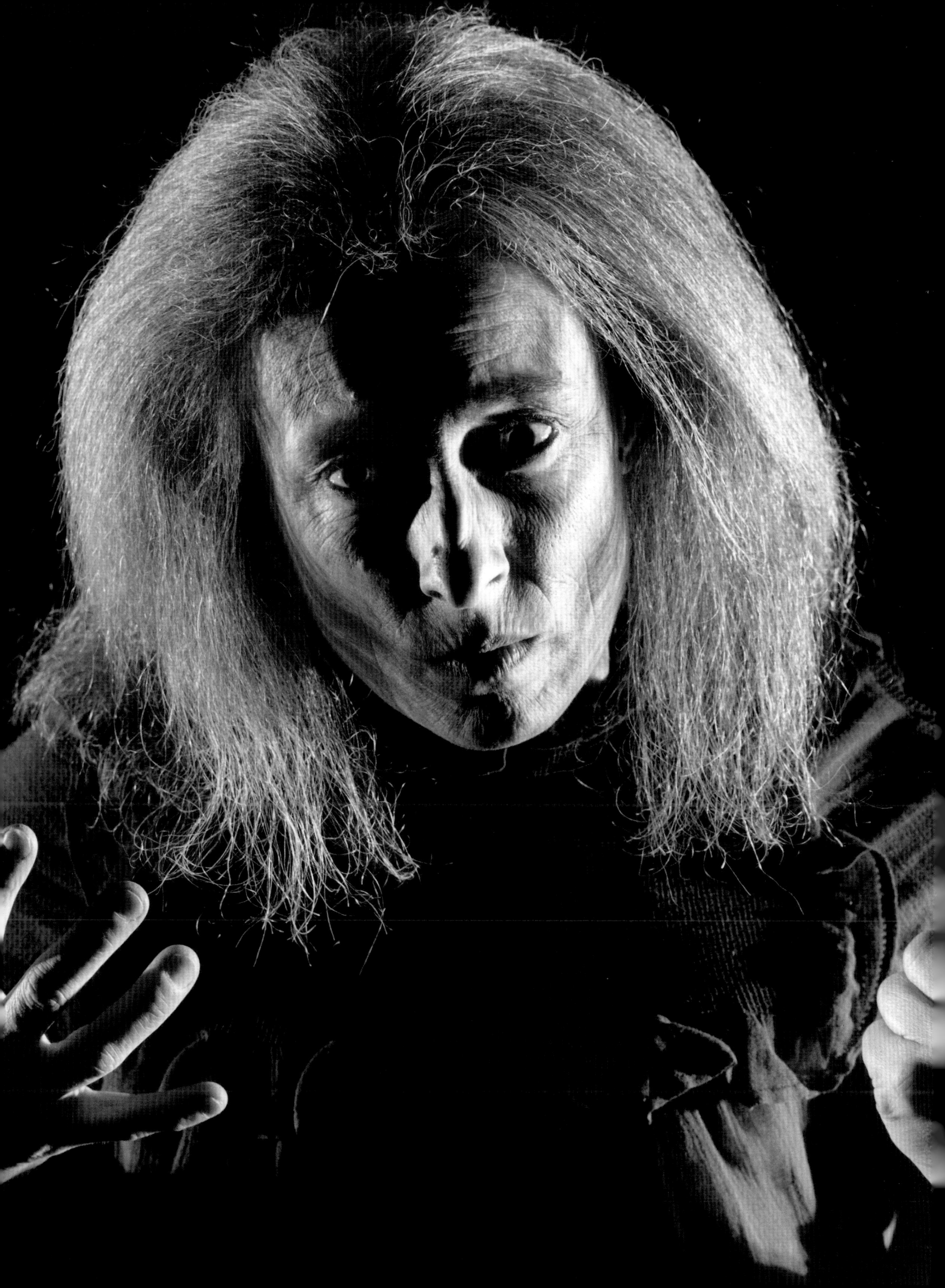

Once drinking deep of that divinest anguish,
How could I seek the empty world again?

EMILY BRONTË, 1818-1848
REMEMBRANCE

PERFORMED BY ELENI KOENKA
1998

Anguish

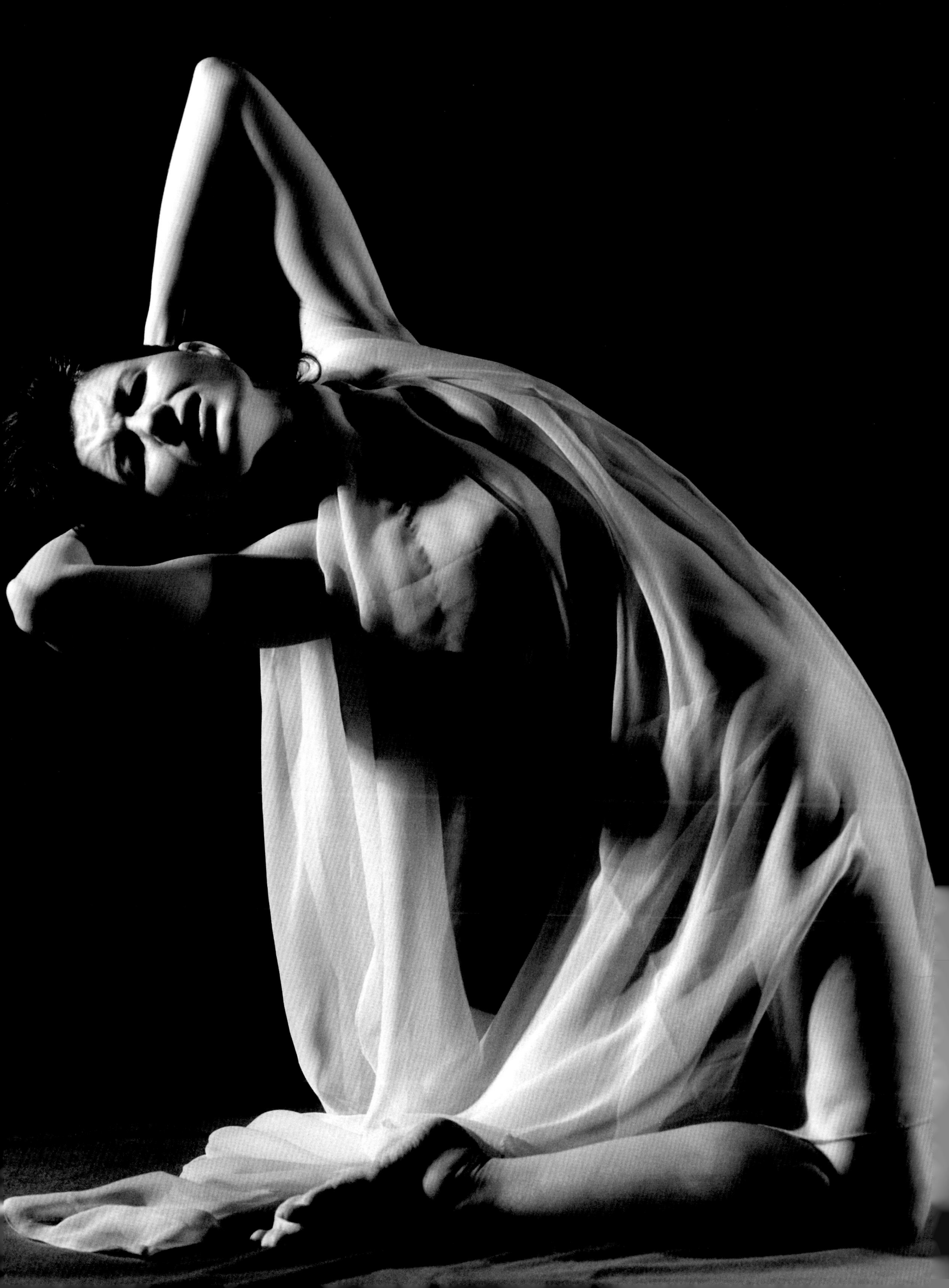

Come then Sorrow! Sweetest Sorrow!
Like an own babe I nurse thee on my breast:
I Thought to leave thee, And deceive thee,
But now of all the world I love thee best.

JOHN KEATS, 1795-1821

PERFORMED BY ANNE SAUVÉ
1992

Sorrow

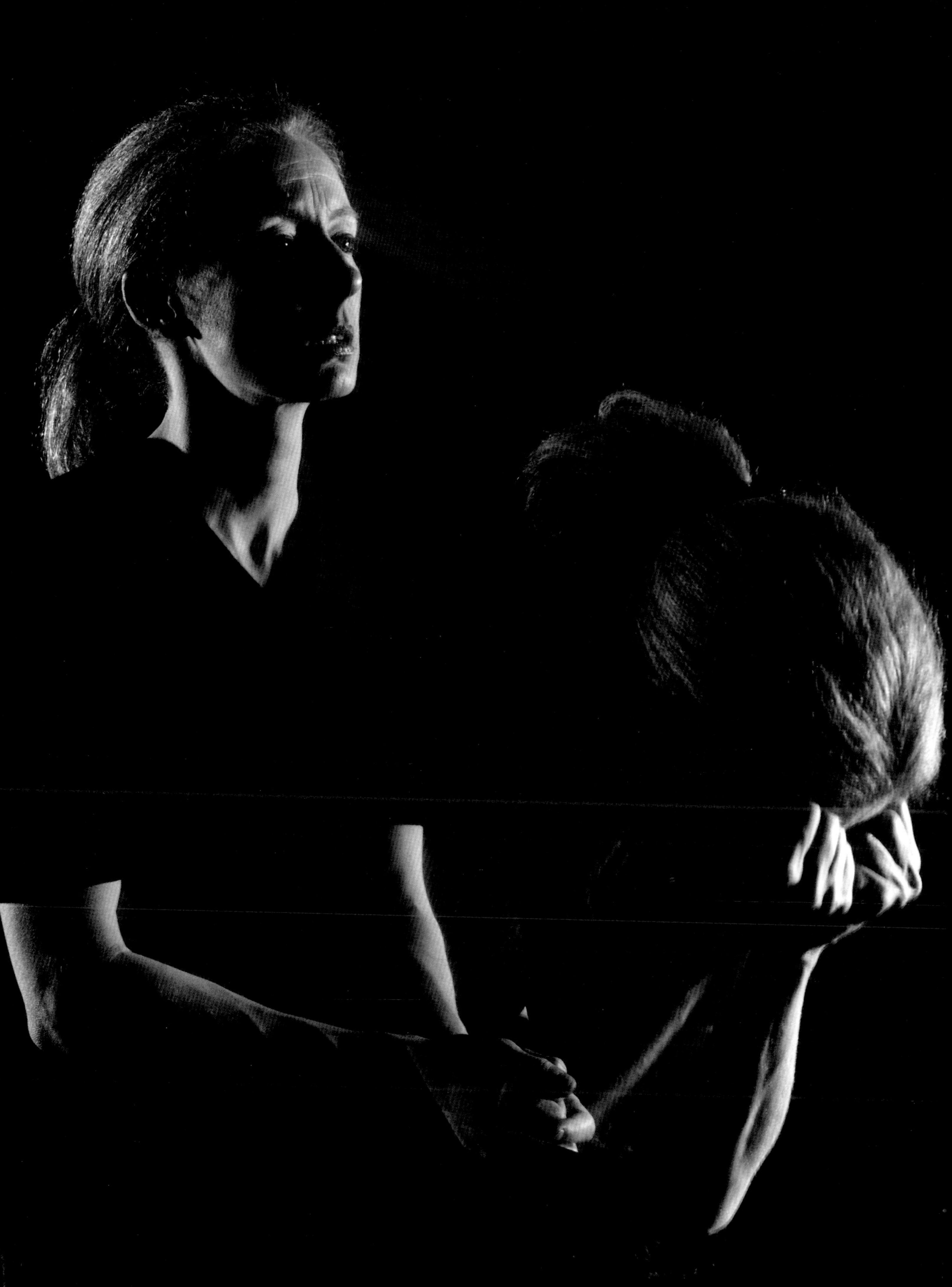

Rest and be thankful

ANONYMOUS
INSCRIPTION ON A STONE BENCH, SCOTLAND

PERFORMED BY ANNE SAUVÉ
1992

Fatigue

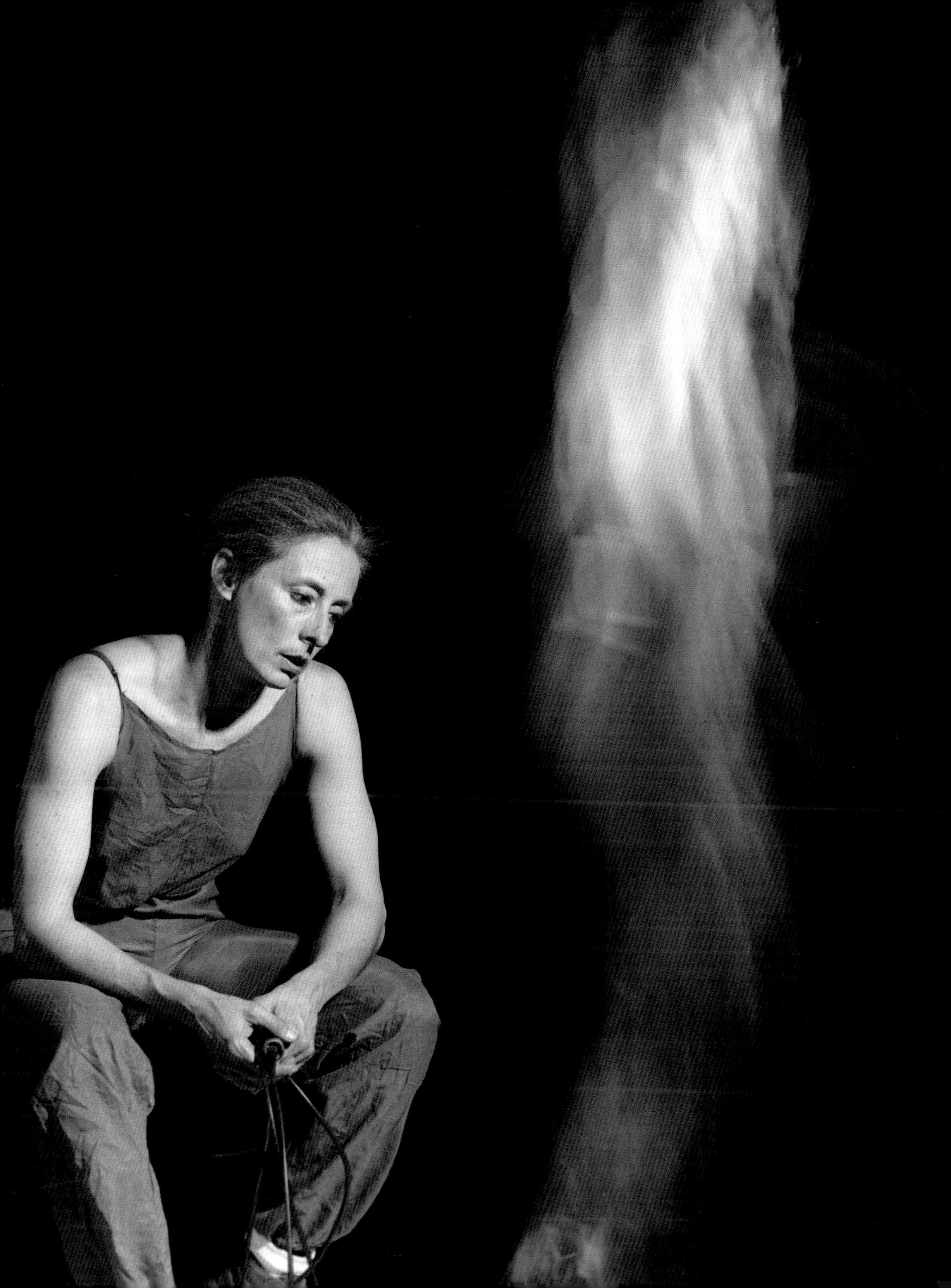

She knew the life-long martyrdom
The weariness, the endless pain
Of waiting for someone to come
Who would never come again.

HENRY WADSWORTH LONGFELLOW, 1807-1882

PERFORMED BY ANNE SAUVÉ
1992

Resignation

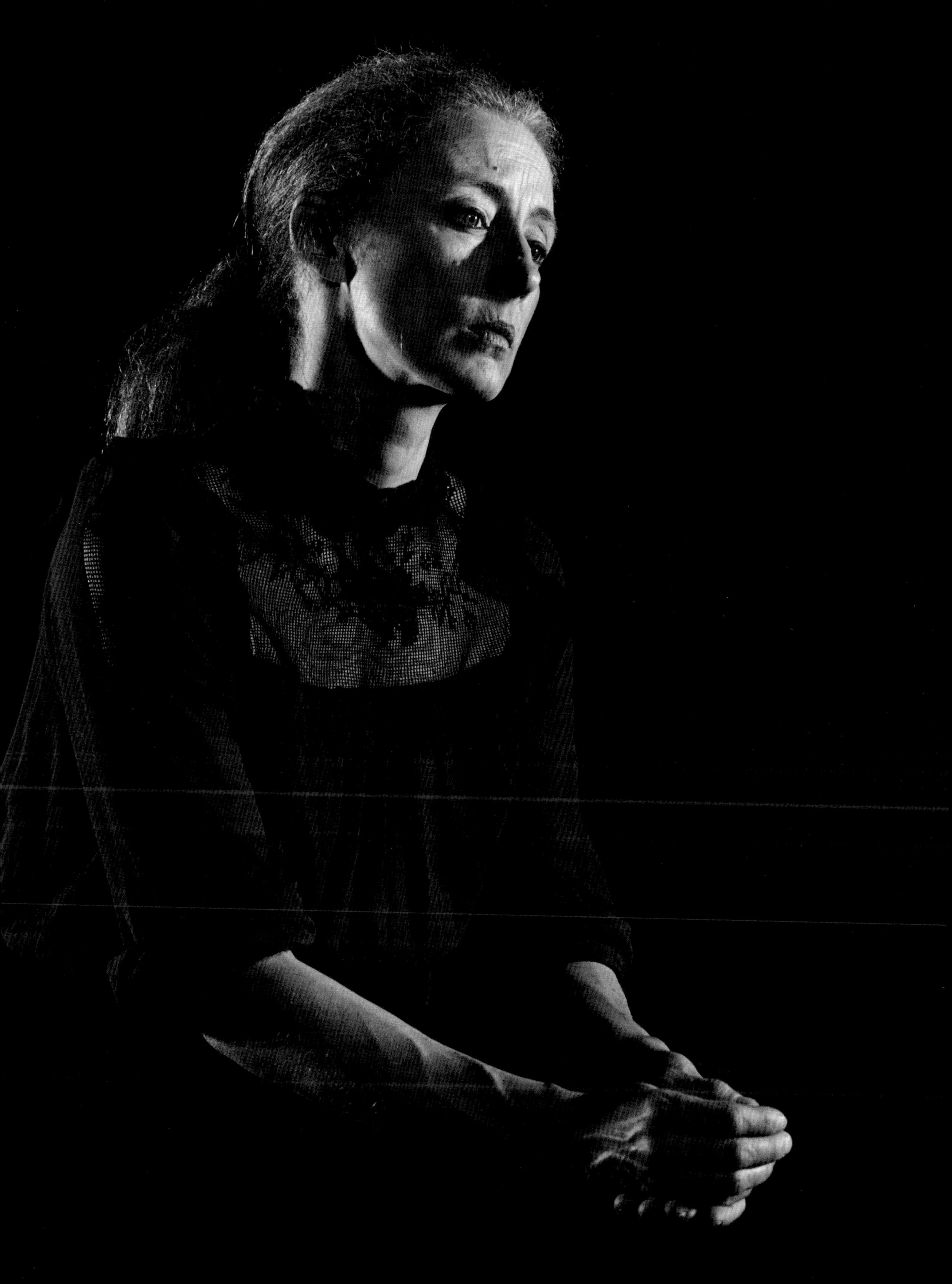

Thanks to the human heart by which we live,
Thanks to its tenderness, its joys and fears,
To me the meanest flower that grows can give
Thoughts that do often lie too deep for tears.

WILLIAM WORDSWORTH, 1770-1850
INTIMATIONS OF IMMORTALITY

PERFORMED BY ELENI KOENKA
1998

Tenderness

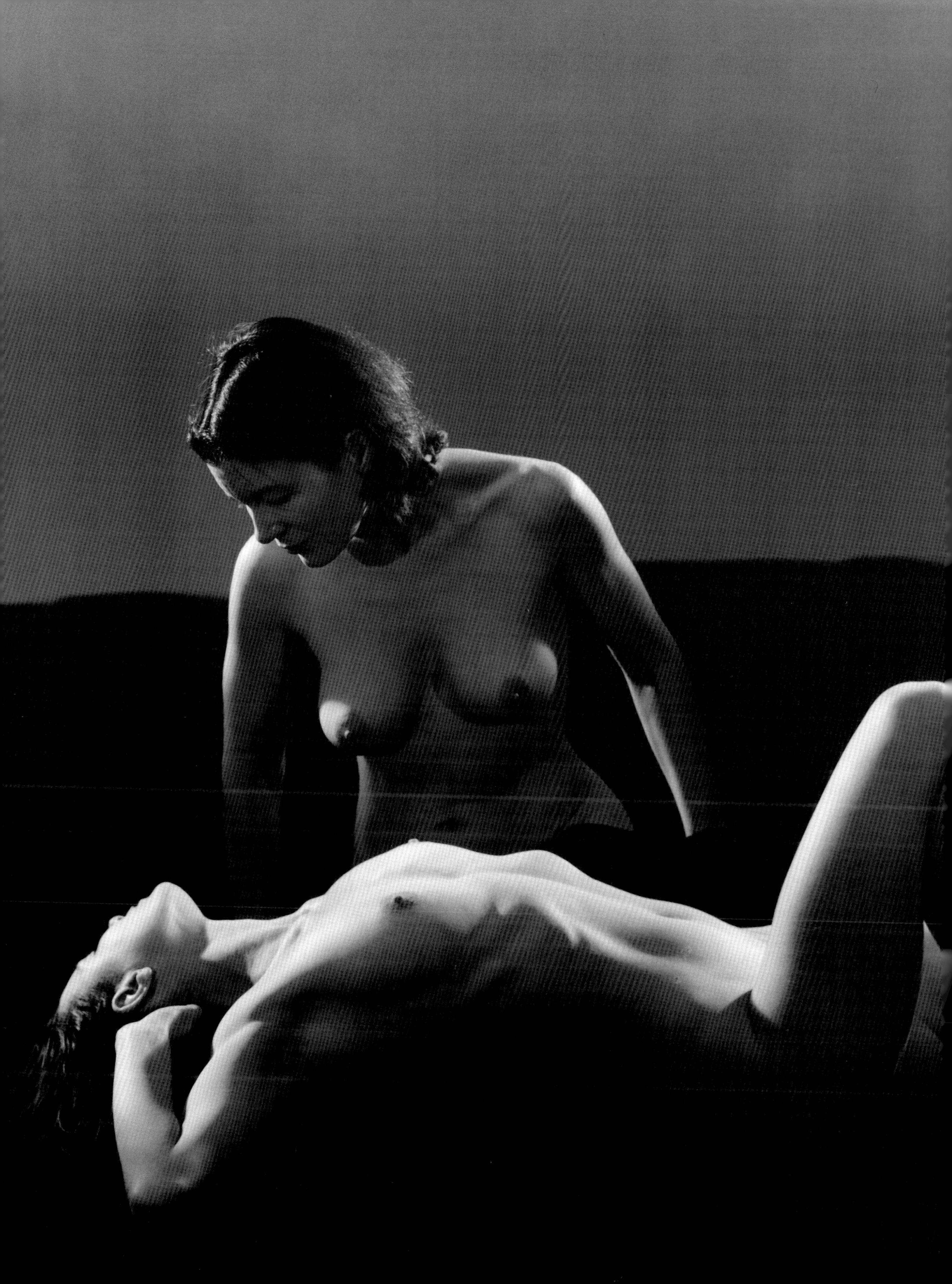

Macavity, Macavity, there's no one like Macavity,
She's broken every human law, she breaks the law
of gravity,
Her powers of levitation would make a fakir stare,
And when you reach the scene of the crime_______
MACAVITY'S NOT THERE!

T.S. ELIOT, 1885-1965
(ADAPTED FOR THE FEMININE GENDER)
OLD POSSUM'S BOOK OF PRACTICAL CATS

PERFORMED BY ELENI KOENKA
1998

Dance of Aggression

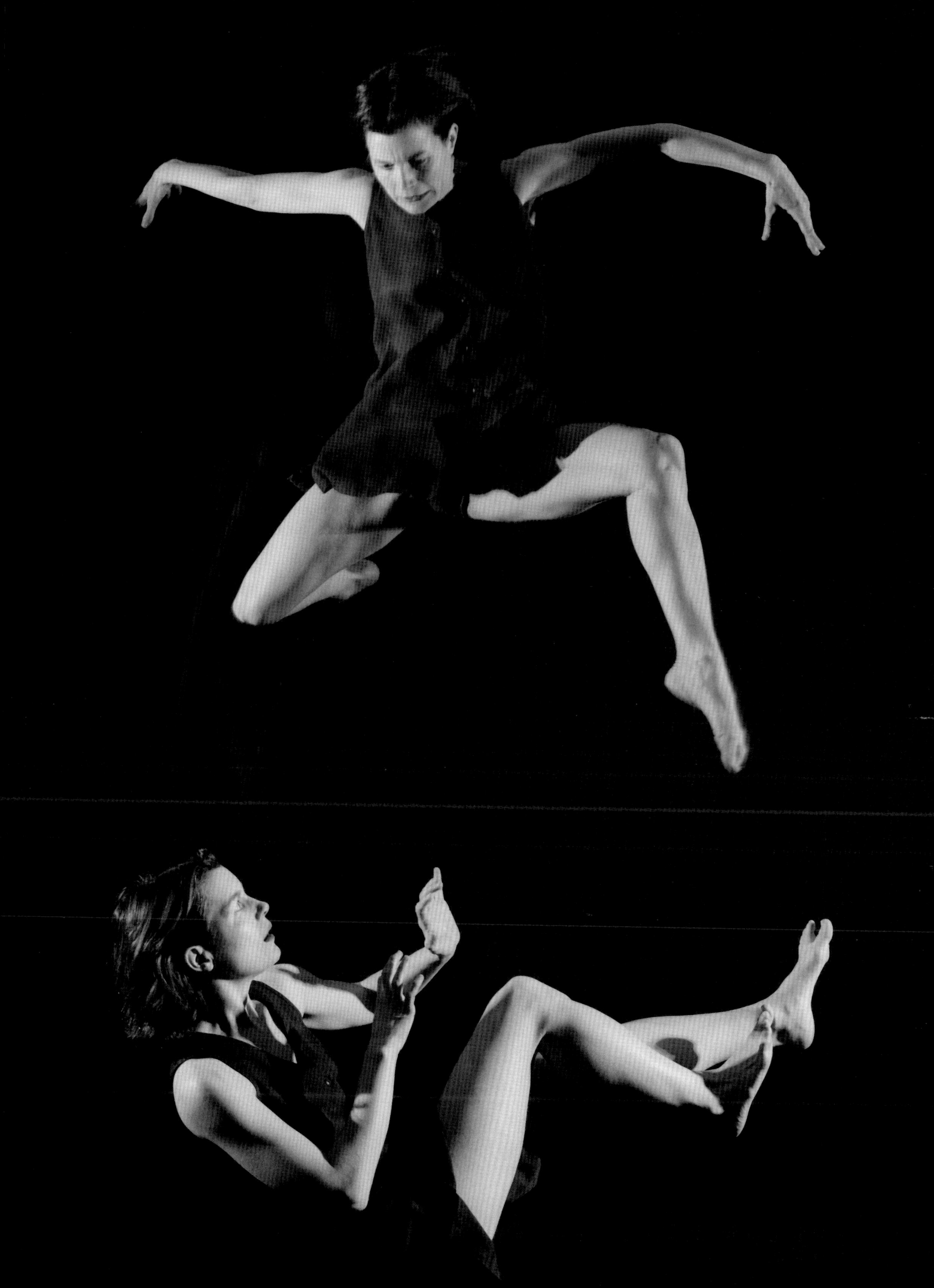

Like a kite
Cut from the string
Lightly the soul of my youth
Has taken flight.

ISHIKAWA TAKUBOKU, 1885-1912
SOUL OF MY YOUTH

PERFORMED BY ELENI KOENKA
1997

Soul of Youth

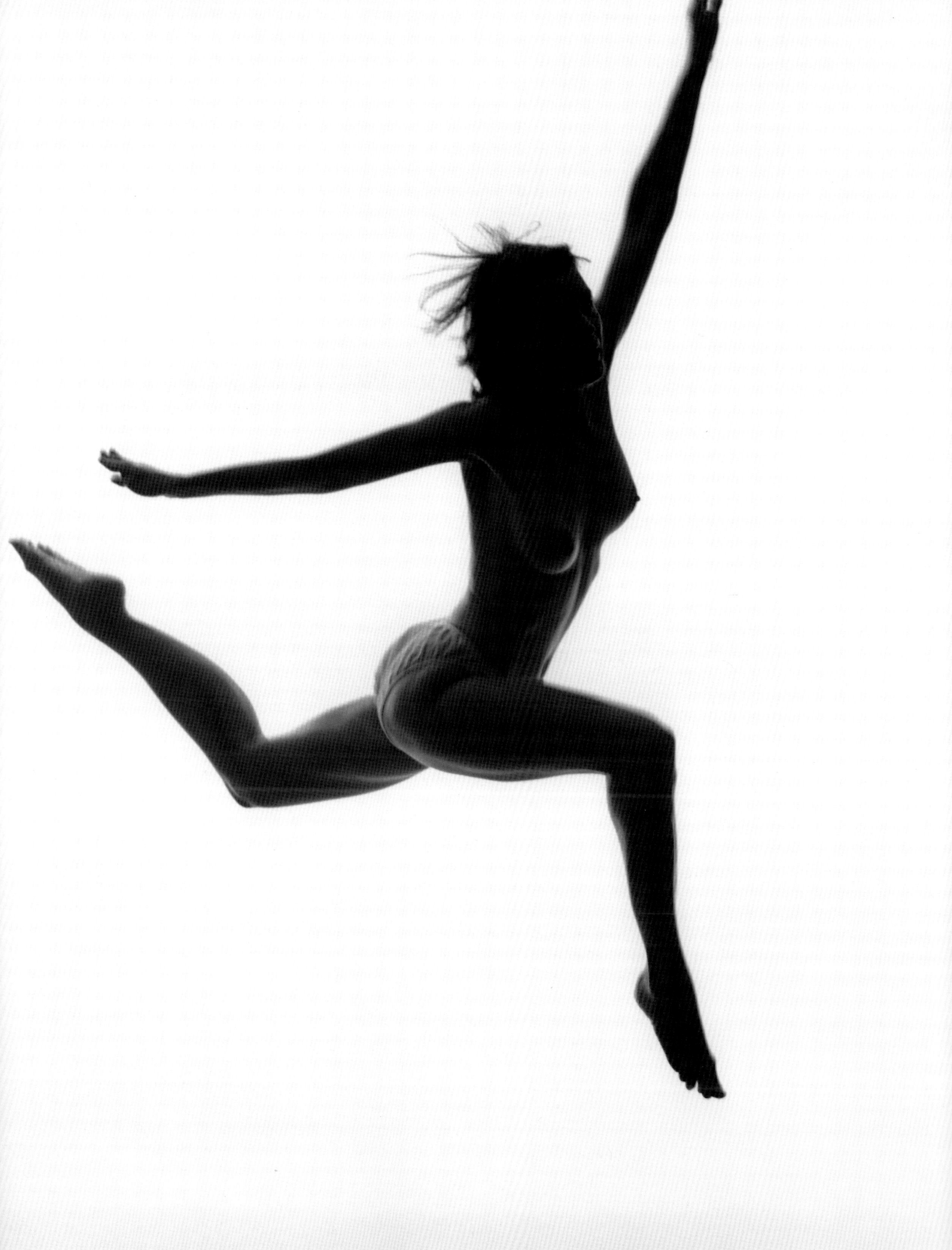

Buffalo gals, won't you come out tonight, won't you come out tonight, won't you come out tonight? Buffalo gals won't you come out tonight, And dance by the light of the moon?

ANONYMOUS
TRADITIONAL SONG REFRAIN

PERFORMED BY SUSAN ABBOTT
1998

Dance by the Light of the Moon

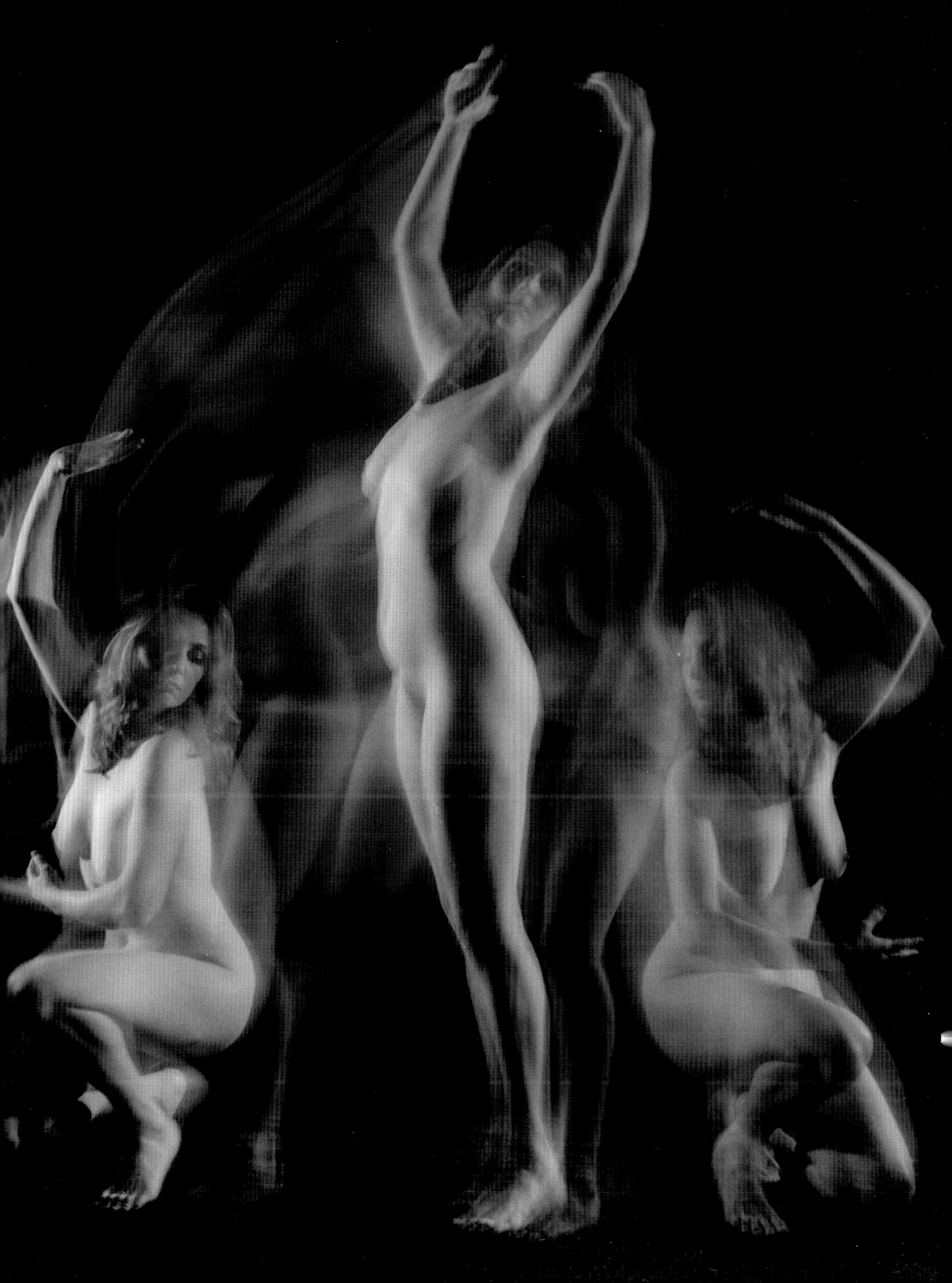

Afterword

HENRY WARD, MD

First impression.... Struck with the power, the.... the what?.... A series of impressions, some that unfolded — complete — some that kept on unfurling.... and the process keeps going on.

Frankly, I had to resist Jim, stop him from telling me what he meant, what he felt, what he wanted me to see because I was too busy seeing for myself. I mention this because it made me think about a conversation I had a half-century ago with the poet, William Carlos Williams. I had been invited to attend a meeting at his home because my college roommate was about to publish one of Williams' poems in a "little mag." As was so characteristic in those days of extreme youth and pretentiousness, I asked Dr. Williams what he thought was the function of art. He turned to me and said without a flicker of hesitation, "Simply to reveal."

In a similar spirit, Jim Mitchell has furnished his readers with a collection of most "revealing" works of art, challenging each viewer/reader with startling "paintings with light on photographic film", paired with equally startling and provocative quotations that create a dialectic, forcing them to arrive at their own individual revelations and creations. As he indicates in the preface, Jim is fully aware that his view, his intent, is only one of a large array of possibilities, some of which he may never imagine himself — and he welcomes them, as well he should, for his success as an artist does not lie in convincing his viewer, but rather with the stimulation, excitement and creation on the part of the viewer that is born from contact with his art.

In representing "emotions and states of being" by the use of this particular medium, Jim has fashioned a richness of ambiguity that is warranted by the various emotions and states of being themselves. I have no doubt that each pairing of picture and quotation will spawn widely varied reactions and interpretations, not just between viewers, but on different occasions with the same viewer. Yet is that not characteristic of emotions themselves? Who ever experiences anger or surprise or shame in exactly the same way twice? And who ever experiences someone else's emotion in a similar way as that person?

Allow me to risk the mischievous suggestion to go through the book again, but this time go from back to front. In other words, see the "light painting" first, immerse yourself in it, then turn to the quotation and roll that around in your brain for a while. Next, go back and forth between the two and let the stew of associations, feelings, spices, and aromas blend to form your own creation. Finally, top it off with Jim's own title and illuminating remarks. I would liken this process to a successful birthing — just as Jim midwifed these pairings, you will have midwifed the fruit of his seed.

There is another revelatory possibility here. Jim Mitchell has provided us with a rich collection of his "children" or creations. They are very intimate and represent a huge part of Jim himself — something one rarely finds in such an immediate and accessible form. It allows us to take the collection and to learn much of who Jim Mitchell is. We can figuratively peer into his skull through his work. Of course, there are as many "Jim Mitchells" as there are those who will take the time and make the effort to distill and integrate this artist from the material he gives us.

For myself, I can only say "thank you, Jim" for the privilege. It still happens each time I go through the book again.

St. George, Maine
December, 1998

Author's Comments

Many of the images in this work can easily stand alone or with the accompanying quotations without additional comment, and this is the way they are presented. Further explanation, however, can be useful to either more fully define the emotion, include some additional verse by other writers, indicate why it was included, or give an indication of the thinking that went into its execution. These comments are noted by image:

Body and Soul

Haven't we all, at one time or other, imagined a scene such as this — the soul leaving the body at the point of death, then going to some better place, always in some visual state such as we would wish to remember them. I have chosen to use this as a starting point for these images. While not an emotion, it is certainly a state of being, or the end of being as we know it, possibly the beginning of being in some other dimension, and it certainly engenders some strong emotions and feelings. The decision to present the scene as death resulting from a road accident came quite easily. Such an accident at night dictates a dark background, making it easier to show a ghost image of the actress's soul emerging from her body. Making the image, though, turned out to be much more difficult than I thought in order to show the soul with just the right amount of transparency as well as indicating its passage from the body.

Contentment

Contentment is normally the calm acquiescence of life, much along the lines of Robert Burns' analogy when he wrote;

> *Contented wi' little, and cantie wi' mair.*

But it can be more, to embrace an outward expression of feeling, one replete with a recognition of the goodness of life. After some discussion we decided to portray the emotion as a scene with the actress waking early in the morning with light beginning to stream into the room. Having her sit and clasp herself with a feeling of pleasure symbolizes the act of embracing life. That it worked is mainly due to the actress's ability.

Serenity

Serenity is a somewhat difficult feeling to know how to portray, largely because it is almost the complete absence of emotion; it is equanimity in the midst of chaos. It wasn't until trying a number of different approaches that I chose to portray the emotion as a woman just emerging from her bath, towel wrapped around her head, not yet clothed, with a chance for quiet and contemplation. Interestingly, the exact same picture but with hair down, and clothed, doesn't work at all.

Surprise

Who has not experienced this emotion of surprise at some point in their lives — the rush of adrenaline, the flushing of the face, the rush to cover up, and the later feeling of embarrassment! It is difficult to remember how many different ways I have attempted to portray this emotion, none very successfully until this image; I suppose because this scene is not only natural but also reminds us of times when we have been in similar circumstances.

Protecting our Inner Self

This is the unseen side of our emotional makeup and has more than one part. On one hand it is the armor that helps us remain calm in the midst of chaos; it is all the lessons learned as we go through childhood and become adults so that our inner fears and weaknesses are not so visible to others. Another side, as beautifully stated by Nora Mitchell, is that we rarely develop the complete trust in another necessary to fully reveal our inner selves, hence we are condemned to live in some degree of loneliness. This image and the first quotation came solely from my imagination. In attempting to demonstrate an enveloping presence as well as a vulnerable inner self, dance-related motion and gestures offered a natural choice.

Pride

The feeling of pride has many origins, with both positive and negative connotations. Its positive side can come from overcoming a difficulty, a sense of achievement, or just self respect. In this vein, John Collins wrote;

> *Though pride is not a virtue, it is the parent of many virtues.*

Pride's negative side is repeated many times in Biblical references, but is also encapsulated quite beautifully by Benedict Spinoza who wrote;

> *Pride is therefore pleasure arising from a man's thinking too highly of himself.*

It was this image, taken fairly early in my association with Eleni, which showed me just how well the use of infrared film seemed to capture her skin tones giving them a depth that does not come through with panchromatic films.

Choice

While choice is not an emotion in itself, it can occasionally involve a great deal of emotional turmoil and courage, such as in choosing a soul mate. Another kind of choice was articulated very cogently by Justice Harry Andrew Blackmun when he wrote in Roe vs. Wade;

> *The right of privacy — is broad enough to encompass a woman's decision*
> *whether or not to terminate a pregnancy.*

This image of a woman mentally choosing which dress to wear is simply a metaphor, albeit a light-hearted one, for all of life's choices.

Abandon

This is defined in the dictionary as; "Unbounded enthusiasm. A complete surrender of inhibitions." I wanted to show this, not in the sense of, "to yield oneself completely to emotion," which is another meaning, but rather in the sense of embracing life fully which requires considerable self confidence. The idea for both the quote and the picture came quite easily; to execute it was another matter which required a number of retakes before the dancer and I were both satisfied.

Joy

To jump for joy is such a strong impulse that you could hardly use another kind of image to portray the emotion. Here is a case where finding the verse first led to defining the image — in this case the use of flying dance steps. The use of a double image was introduced to reinforce the impact.

Grace

There are ambiguities in this image which to me are part of its charm. It could be flirtation or even modesty, and yet she is certainly bold. Beyond these, however, there is a definite combination of beauty, symmetry, and gracefulness in her movements. Although this image was made separately from finding John Cheever's verse, they seem to belong together. Several well known photographers have made images similar to this. The difference is in the film, the lighting, and the beauty of the dancer. This, one of my favorite dance pictures, uses infrared film with strobe lighting almost entirely to the rear — a combination which works very well with the dancer's skin — both for its softness and luminosity, as well as backlit strobes for its power.

Seduction

While we can be lured by many things to pursue something more desirable than that which duty demands, we normally think of seduction in a more sexual sense. The art, of course, is to carry it off with class and to remain a lady in the process! How many times have I attempted to capture the essence of seduction on film without it being either too obvious or too obtuse. It helps, of course, to work with a beautiful young woman, but that alone is no guarantee of success. In this quite classic pose, the actress has performed it with just the right touch of suggestion and acquiescence without being overt. She remains every inch the lady, fitting well with Aphra Behn's quotation.

Passion

We can be passionate about many things and display this in anger, speech, or action. We normally think of it, however, in the more sexual sense. To me passion involves fairly violent movement combined with intense emotion. Photographically this means using an open shutter to capture some essence of motion combined with the use of strobes to freeze the action and reveal the figures. The problem is to accomplish all this without losing too much in the quality of the image — a somewhat difficult juggling act.

Submission

Is she pleading, cajoling, or submitting? Or is it all three? We can't know exactly, nor can we know which came first. But in this case the ambiguity seems to lend extra power to the image. It is the same ambiguity as developed in John Milton's verse; both seem to reflect the ability of many women to achieve their goals through indirect means.

Adoration

The primary definition of adoration is; "the worship of God or a godlike figure." The emotion can be carried further into a form of ecstasy which in this case is defined as; "the trance, frenzy, or rapture associated with mystic or prophetic exaltation." In this scene the mime actress develops both adoration and ecstasy as the final image, but it was highlighted by strobe at the point of adoration where she was still in control of her actions. Photographed with an open shutter over a rather long exposure of eight seconds, the picture has a mystical quality, befitting the emotion.

Ecstasy

The dictionary definition is; "a state of emotion so intense that one is carried beyond rational thought and self control." Intense emotion cries out strongly for extremes in posture and lighting. These combined with infrared film were used to reveal little more than the planes and muscles of the actress's face and neck with no attempt to soften or accentuate her feminine nature.

Rejection

There are situations and emotional scenes where body language seems to speak more eloquently than words, and I believe this is one of them. The acting of the standing figure, with the throw of the hip, speaks volumes as does the appearance of remorse on the part of the seated figure. The only incongruity is that both are the same person.

Regret

Regret is a form of sadness, less strong than melancholy but more than resignation. It is a form of longing, usually fairly fleeting, for something that didn't work out the way one hoped. In this image, taken in a garment which would only be worn in private, the overall scene works well with Sarah Orne Jewett's verse.

Melancholy

Melancholy has many faces, both sweet and sad. It can be pensive reflection and contemplation with a drawing into oneself. It can be a lingering sadness; yet it can be charming or sweet as in these lines by Robert Burton;

All my joys to this are folly / Naught so sweet as melancholy.

This portrayal by the dancer/actress, using gestures which come largely from dance, captures both the flavor of the emotion and some of its nuances. It is pensive without being overly sad; it is contained and inward looking. Yet it is far from being a depressing emotion.

Anger

While anger may start in the brain, it is felt first in the pit of the stomach. This mime portrayal shows both full flowering of the emotion as well as its beginning — eloquently stated in a verse by Robert Burns;

> *Where sits our sullen sulky dame,*
> *Gathering her brows like a gathering storm,*
> *Nursing her wrath to keep it warm.*

Hate

Even though I took this image of the actress/dancer, Eleni, it is still difficult to realize that it is the same person who acted out such emotions as *Joy, Contentment,* or *Tenderness.* How many facial expressions can one young woman achieve? How can a very pretty person look so fierce? I believe the secret may lie in the fact that for this instant at least she was not acting, but reliving some ancient, learned hatreds. Eleni grew up in Greece where her family suffered under German occupation during World War II. While she herself wasn't born at the time, she grew up with all the stories and the absorbed hatreds. So when I mentioned the word "Nazis", it triggered the emotional fervor to facilitate this photograph. The use of lighting and film to minimize her normal femininity certainly helped, but it is her ability to portray emotion that makes the picture work.

Fear

The dictionary defines fear as; "Fear is the most general term covering fright, dread, terror, horror, panic, alarm, dismay, or several other related conditions. It is the feeling of agitation, sometimes severe, caused by the presence or imminence of danger." The extreme fear described by Shakespeare is acted out in this multiple exposure. In this case I used the image of the actress on the ground to reflect his phrase;

> *But coward-like with trembling terror die.*

The placement of this image in the midsection of the upright figure was also deliberate; it is often here in the pit of the stomach where the emotion is felt most strongly, as in the expression "sick with fear".

Shame, Despair, Solitude

These are all powerful, negative emotional states. Shame carries a sense of guilt and unworthiness; despair is the utter lack of hope, the blackest of holes; solitude in this case infers complete isolation. As Rudyard Kipling wrote about despair;

> *It is an emotion which might find*
> *expression in — suicide.*

The combination of all three of these emotions in Nathaniel Hawthorne's lines must have been meant to show total emotional devastation; it is reflected here by the mime actress sinking into a posture of total dejection.

There is another quotation by John Milton which treats despair eloquently;

Me miserable! which way shall I fly
Infinite wrath, and infinite despair?
Which way I fly is hell; myself am hell;
And in the lowest deep a lower deep,
Still threat'ning to devour me, open wide,
To which the hell I suffer seems a heaven.

Grief

Grief is beyond sadness; it is deep mental distress arising from bereavement. It is handled in different ways by different people and manifests itself differently over time. In this image the mime acting is meant to match William Shakespeare's stark lines from Romeo and Juliet. The final lines from Act V are equally powerful;

For never a story of more woe
Than this of Juliet and her Romeo.

Madness

The emotional extremes expressed in Emily Dickinson's verse are reflected in this powerful, almost shocking portrayal by the mime actress. At the same time some ambiguities seem apparent. Is it sense? Is it anger? Is it madness? Or is it that she just can't seem to make us understand? We can't know, but the conflicts and frustrations seem evident — the piercing gaze, the pursed mouth, even the hands, one open, and the other clenched.

Anguish

The agony and torment of anguish are so evident in this dance portrayal that words are hardly necessary. Virginia Woolf expressed another very personal view of this emotion when she wrote;

The beauty of the world has two edges, one
of laughter, one of anguish, cutting the heart asunder.

Sorrow

Sorrow is another emotion related to sadness; it is a more outward expression of mental suffering than melancholy; it is less intense than grief. Like melancholy it can be persistent, but it can become comforting as described in the verse by John Keats.

Fatigue

All of us experience this feeling at various times, and not just from physical exertion. It can also result from serious mental effort. But how do we make it seem real in a photograph? While the mime actress is perfectly capable of portraying fatigue through her posture and expression alone, this is an instance where we both felt the impact would be heightened by showing a ghost image of her jumping rope as the cause of the feeling. Thus this image is an example of an open shutter picture to describe the activity followed by a still portrait of her in a fatigued state, using separate lighting entirely. As a side note on the quotation, some references ascribe it to a poem by William Wordsworth. My examination of his works, however, revealed no evidence of such poem, or line in a poem, hence the credit as shown.

Resignation

Resignation is just that — the unresisting acceptance of the inevitable. There may be sadness for what might have been, but less than in regret. Longfellow's verse is an eloquent statement but possibly tends more toward real regret than another wonderful quote by John Cowper Powys which says it differently;

> *That tender compromise called resignation is only an eloquent name for the dying down, the wearing thin, of the vital impulses in us.*

Except for the actress's expression and body language, this image probably comes closer than any other in this body of work to a true portrait.

Tenderness

It seems most fitting that this, one of the gentlest of all emotions, be portrayed as if between two women. Here they are even closer emotionally than identical twins, they are the same person. The image comes purely from the imagination as a comforting moment set against an evening sky, although actually executed in the studio. Of all the images in this book, this was undoubtedly the most challenging and most difficult to achieve in the studio. It contains two separate images of the same actress, not only on the same negative, but overlapping. It also required that they have eye contact and be communicating emotionally. An added complication was to portray the scene as if there was an evening sky in the background.

Dance of Aggression

Like two cats at play, like many sports, or just like life in general, there are often aggressive moves matched by defensive stances. Then the roles may become reversed. This enactment is based on a dance interpretation with one dancer acting both roles. As in many of these photographs where one actress plays two roles with a double image recorded on the same negative, a number of attempts were required to achieve the desired result. To me the final result not only demonstrates an almost perfect dance jump, but also shows both a fierce countenance and excellent eye contact between the two dancers.

Soul of Youth

I believe this is an almost perfect example of what Man Ray meant when he wrote;

> *Photography is*
> *a marvelous explorer*
> *of aspects that our retina*
> *will never register.*

She really is a kite, cut loose and soaring. Only a camera can capture and record that perfect moment of the dancer's art, in the air, flying, before it is gone and she has landed to assume some still point that we can see long enough to register and remember. Yet it is motion and grace like this that captures our imagination and provides much of the emotional impact of dance as described in Havelock Ellis' quotation;

> *Dancing is the loftiest, the most moving, the most*
> *beautiful of the arts, because it is no mere translation*
> *or abstraction from life; it is life itself.*

Although this picture emulates flight against the sky, it was actually accomplished in the studio by aiming strobes at a neutral background and positioning the dancer so that only a small amount of reflected light registered on her body.

Dance by the Light of the Moon

T. S. Eliot once wrote;

> *Except for the point, the still point,*
> *There would be no dance, and there is only*
> *the dance.*

I have no quarrel with this. It is the still points of dance that we see and retain in our memories. The movements of dance, which lend it its grace, beauty, and emotional content, do not register as well or long enough through our eyes to remember with clarity. Yet without these and music to provide rhythm and melody, dance would be more like unconnected statues, devoid of real life. The previous image which captures the motion only and this image which combines still points with at least the ghosts of motion, is my effort to show the combined power of the dance. The dance itself is intended to depict the emergence, dance, and retreat of the dancer, and is timed to match the length of the refrain.

On Making These Images

The choice of infrared film for about a third of the images in this book was based on two major considerations. As stated by Walter Pater in the Quotations; "It is the addition of strangeness to beauty that constitutes the romantic character in art." Because infrared film sees colors differently than we do, it accentuates the blackness of the eye, lightens the lips, and produces a more sculptural look to the body than normal panchromatic films. Because infrared film is also sensitive to heat, it tends to provide a luminosity to the skin. These in combination with "proper" exposure add a kind of strangeness, beautiful but different, to the human figure. Whether it be the image of *Contentment, Pride, Grace, Ecstasy, Grief,* or *Anguish*, to name a few, each has a somewhat otherworldly look.

Another characteristic of this film is that it tends to smooth out both skin and contours of the body, so that with certain choices of lighting, you see far less detail than normal. In other words, it encourages you to concentrate on the more important elements of the image.

Multiple figures on the same negative account for almost half of the images in this book. Some of these were quite difficult to achieve successfully for several reasons. As in the image of *Abandon* each figure had to be photographed at just that perfect moment of motion, position, and expression. Thus with three figures, the odds against having all three come out perfectly went up exponentially. Second, with widely separated figures, it was a challenge to maintain more or less even light intensity. Third, lights had to be located so that no stray light hit the background, and very little reflected from the floor. The solution was repeated retakes. Therefore, after completing a photo session and making work prints, these were reviewed with the actress/dancer, adjustments made, and another group of pictures were taken. Then the process was repeated, sometimes several times, until it finally came out right.

From a purely technical standpoint, the most challenging of these multiple images was *Tenderness.* Here, you not only had two figures which had to be emotionally engaged with each other, but also they had to overlap each other without allowing a reflection of light on the rear figure to come through as a ghost image. Additionally, I wanted some light on the background to simulate an evening sky.

Finally, almost one third of the images in this book used an open shutter for all or part of the total picture. The purpose was to show ghost images of motion deliberately to add impact or credence to the total scene. Most like *Surprise* or *Adoration* involved a combination of flood lights for the motion and strobes to stop action at a particular point. In the final picture in the book, however, *Dance by the Light of the Moon*, only flood lights were used both for the motion and the stopped action to give the picture a somewhat mystical look, as if it had actually been taken by moonlight.

Order Memorandum

To: PLEASANT VIEW PRESS
120 Barnestown Road
P.O. Box 778
Camden, Maine 04843
Telephone: (207) 236-2998

Via Fax: (207) 236-0677
or
E-Mail: pvpress@mint.net

From: ______________________________
____
____

Fax: ____________________________
or
E-Mail: __________________________

Date: ______________________________

I would like to order ______ additional copy/ies of the hard cover *First Edition* of ***Body & Soul*** by James Andrew Mitchell at the publisher's price of $40.00 per copy. A shipping cost of $2. 00 will be added within the United States outside of the state of Maine. No shipping cost will apply to orders within the state but a $2.00 charge will be made to cover sales tax

.

I would like to order the following *Limited Edition Print/s* from the book as described in the AVAILABILITY OF PRINTS description by title:

________________________________, __________________________________

________________________________, __________________________________.

My check for $__________ is enclosed,

or bill my VISA/ MC No: ______________________________
Expiration date: ______________________________
telephone no. ______________________________,

or contact my Bookstore: ______________________________
____
____

whose telephone number is: ______________________________ .

Please respond as quickly as possible.

Body & Soul

AVAILABILITY OF PRINTS

A limited edition of photographs by James Andrew Mitchell is available for selected images from which the book was produced. Each of these is 11" by 14", dry mounted on 16" by 20" bright white archival board, and matted. All photographs are black and white silver prints, selenium toned for archival permanence, printed on *Forte Elegance* exhibition paper from Hungary. The edition is limited to an issue of ten prints each, signed, numbered, and dated, of the following images as they are titled in the book:

- ☐ ***Abandon*** performed by Eleni Koenka, 1997
- ☐ ***Anguish*** performed by Eleni Koenka, 1998
- ☐ ***Body & Soul*** performed by Eleni Koenka, 1998
- ☐ ***Choice*** performed by Susan Abbott, 1998
- ☐ ***Contentment*** performed by Eleni Koenka, 1998
- ☐ ***Dance by the Light of the Moon*** performed by Susan Abbott, 1998
- ☐ ***Ecstasy*** performed by Susan Abbott, 1998
- ☐ ***Fatigue*** performed by Anne Sauve, 1992
- ☐ ***Grace*** performed by Eleni Koenka, 1997
- ☐ ***Joy*** performed by Eleni Koenka, 1997
- ☐ ***Protecting our Inner Self*** performed by Eleni Koenka, 1998
- ☐ ***Resignation*** performed by Anne Sauve, 1992
- ☐ ***Shame, Despair, Solitude*** performed by Marguerite Mathews, 1992
- ☐ ***Soul of Youth*** performed by Eleni Koenka, 1997
- ☐ ***Tenderness*** performed by Eleni Koenka, 1998

The price for each print, numbered and signed, is $350. including shipping, any applicable taxes, and a royalty payment to the performing artist. A boxed portfolio of any ten of these prints is available for $3,000.

Requests for individual prints not included in this group will be considered by the publisher. To order or request further information please contact;

PLEASANT VIEW PRESS
P.O. Box 778, Camden, Maine 04843
Telephone 207-236-2998, Facsimile 207-236-0677, E-Mail pvpress @ mint.net